THE AMAZING KID'S BOOK OF ASTROLOGY & CONSTELLATIONS!

THE BEGINNER'S GUIDE TO OUTER SPACE, LEGENDARY TALES OF THE STARS, PLUS INTERESTING FACTS FOR JUNIOR ASTROLOGERS & ASTRONOMERS AGED 8 TO 12!

ANIELA PUBLICATIONS

ANIELA
publications

CONTENTS

ASTROLOGY FOR KIDS

CONSTELLATIONS FOR KIDS

ASTROLOGY FOR KIDS

THE FUN WAY TO LEARN STAR SIGNS, MASTER THE ZODIAC, AND DISCOVER YOUR POTENTIAL FUTURE!

CHAPTER 1
WELCOME TO THE AMAZING WORLD OF ASTROLOGY!

Thousands of years ago, people believed that the stars in the night sky had special powers. Just like the gods could make changes to your life, everyone thought that the stars could influence people to behave in certain ways. It might sound strange to us now, but back then, it made perfect sense. They already knew that the sun changed the temperature and brought light to the world. They also knew that the moon could control the tides and make the oceans move. So, why wouldn't the stars also control things?

A long time ago, people looking up at the night sky noticed that there were patterns in the stars! They also paid attention and realized that these patterns moved across the night sky, but they always appeared in the same place on the same dates. So these observant people created astrology: an amazing tool to help them navigate the skies and pay attention to what the stars and planets are doing!

Astrologers believe that people on earth can be affected by the position of the stars way up above and that astrology can even tell us about events happening down here on earth. Ancient astrologers separated the year into 12 different pieces, each piece based on a different pattern in the sky. They called these patterns constellations and organized them in a circle they called the zodiac. These 12 pieces are known as Capricorn, Aquarius, Pisces, Aries, Taurus, Gemini, Cancer, Leo, Virgo, Libra, Scorpio, and Sagittarius.

The zodiac shows twelve different signs—sometimes called star signs—and these signs have a strong influence for about 30 days every year. Astrologers believe that each sign can determine what a person will be like if they are born under its influence. They spent years studying the people around them and spotted the similarities in people who were born under the same sign. These traits became the basis for the different star sign personalities.

· · ·

Astrology isn't a strict set of personality traits that won't change, but rather a fun way to have a sense of belonging and understanding of things that make us so unique! There are so many things that determine the way we act, feel, or express ourselves. Things like culture, experiences, who our friends are, and so on. So remember, astrology can be a fun way to find out what kind of traits you might share with others that have the same zodiac sign (or even a different sign, for that matter!) You might find yourself saying things like, "I can't help being a bright light in the room; I'm a Leo!" or "Wow! My best friend is so helpful—he's a typical Taurus.

A LOOK INTO THE PAST—WHERE DID ASTROLOGY BEGIN?

Historians think that some form of astrology has been around since we were all living in caves! Cave paintings are simple pieces of art that have been drawn on or carved into the stone walls of caves and mountains. Researchers in charge of studying them have noticed that some of the animals drawn in the paintings are not actually animals at all—they are actually showing the animal constellations in the night sky!

These cave paintings show us that early humans were using the positions of the stars to show the dates of important events like a comet hitting the Earth. Some of these cave paintings are 40,000 years old! Humans have been looking up at the stars for a very long time, and most of them are the same stars that we see today.

THE CONSTELLATIONS

The patterns that people see in the night sky are called constellations. They are groups of stars that can be joined up with an imaginary line to make a picture. Some of these constellations have been found in cave paintings, meaning they are very old. Taurus the Bull was being painted on walls as far back in time as the Bronze Age! (The Bronze Age can be described as the years between 3300 to 1200 B.C., approximately. This is the time when humans invented the wheel and started working with metals!)

Because ancient people could always rely on the constellations being up in the sky, they used them to keep track of time and the months. Just like how you might have a calendar on your cell phone, ancient people used the constellations as a sort of calendar in the sky.

Each star sign in the zodiac is named after a different constellation. Most of them are animals, but others are people or objects that appeared in popular Greek myths.

ASTROLOGY IN ANCIENT CIVILIZATIONS

Cave humans may have been finding patterns in the stars and using them to track dates, but it wasn't until much later that ancient astrologers began to organize this thinking into proper systems. What is really interesting is that people in different countries all over the world were seeing similar pictures and making the same calculations all by themselves.

BABYLONIAN ASTROLOGY

Babylonia was part of Mesopotamia, a large area in the modern-day Middle East. Their astrologers would use the position of the stars and planets to predict the seasons and decide the best time for sowing, harvesting, hunting, and fishing. This was important information for keeping everybody fed and healthy. Babylonian astrologers divided the year into twelve different sections that would later become the signs of the zodiac.

The Babylonians were also big believers in omens. Omens are signs that can tell something good or bad is about to happen. They spotted many of these omens in the stars and would use them to predict big changes.

GREEK ASTROLOGY

The Greeks spent lots of their time invading other countries, and when they did, they would learn about the countries' technology and science. Alexander the Great, an important Greek ruler, invaded Babylonia and brought the secrets of astrology back to Greece. With added information from Greek astrologers, a new form of astrology was born—one that used your star sign to create a horoscope that could make predictions about your life.

EGYPTIAN ASTROLOGY

Astrology in Egypt developed differently from Babylonia. The Egyptians were more interested in recording a regular cycle of stars, so they divided the year into 36 different parts called decans. Each part was signaled by the appearance of a new star. When the Egyptians were invaded by the Greeks, they shared this information with them. The Greeks realized that the decans matched up with their zodiac signs if they grouped them into threes.

The Egyptians also linked their decans to the four different natural elements: earth, air, fire, and water. These are still associated with the different star signs today and have become an important part of Western astrology.

WESTERN ASTROLOGY

All the contributions from these different civilizations eventually led to what we use in astrology today. Western astrology has twelve signs of the zodiac that are arranged in a wheel. This makes it really easy to see the signs that are opposite each other, as well as the signs that are next to each other. Each sign influences the same dates every year, making it really easy to identify your star sign.

Western astrology uses lots of different elements when making a prediction about a person. It looks at their birth sign as well as where the planets were on the day that they were born. This is because Western astrology treats the Earth and everything on it as one single life form, so we are all affected by the same changes that take place.

In Western astrology, each star sign has its own ruling planet. These planets are associated with personality traits and skills that the planet will share with people born under its influence. Each sign is also associated with a natural element. Those signs that share the same element have common likes and behaviors that mean they will get on well with each other.

THE CHINESE ZODIAC

It wasn't just in Europe and the Middle East where astrology was popular; Chinese astrologers had developed their own system at a very similar time. Chinese astrology is different from western astrology because it has one sign for the whole year. Their signs are all named after different animals, but there are still twelve of them. Every twelve years, the cycle repeats itself.

MODERN ASTROLOGY

Astrology was a really important part of life for people in Europe and Asia for many centuries. Rich people would pay to have their horoscopes read by astrologers and would use this information to make decisions about their life. Even kings and queens would decide battle plans or who to marry based on information from the stars. It was common for royalty to have a court astrologer who was in charge of keeping them updated about lucky times and good omens.

By the end of the 18th century, scientists started spreading the word that there were perhaps more logical explanations for events and that astrology might not be super accurate! This meant that lots of people stopped relying on astrology to tell them things like how the weather would be and where they should build their temples.

Even though some people during this time stopped believing in astrology, there are still countless people today that believe in astrology and use it for lots of different things.

Today, people are far more open to different beliefs, and astrology has returned. We know that science can prove some things, but it cannot disprove others. This means that ancient ideas, including astrology and alternative medicines, have never been proven to be right or wrong. People will make use of these things if they want to. Some people are very serious in their beliefs, while others find astrology to be a resource they can interpret loosely.

How you want to use the information in this book is entirely up to you!

CHAPTER 2
FUN STAR SIGN FACTS

Before you go looking up your own star sign, let's have a look at some fun facts about all the different signs. Do you know which star sign has given us the most US Presidents? One fun sign has produced more child actors than any other, and yet another sign is more likely to become a billionaire when they grow up! Maybe this will be a little look into your own future. After all, people often say that your future is written in the stars.

More of the world's top athletes were born with the star sign Aquarius than any other. This includes current sports stars as well as the historical greats from all sorts of different sports. Muhammed Ali, Michael Jordan, and the great Babe Ruth all shared this star sign, so it must be pretty great to be an Aquarius.

Pisces are among the happiest people on the planet, especially at work. They enjoy their jobs more than most of the other signs. Maybe that's because they pick their careers carefully, or maybe they just enjoy feeling useful and being able to make a difference.

Aries are the most careful drivers and follow the rules of the road—so the only tickets they will be getting are from the arcade! But that doesn't mean they're always slow: legendary race car drivers Jacques Villeneuve and Ayrton Senna were born under the Aries sign, and nobody could accuse them of being slow behind the wheel!

Do you find yourself reciting lots of memorized facts and impressing your friends? You could be a Taurus; they are known for having the most amazing memory. Those who are born under the sign of Taurus enjoy retaining huge amounts of information, so they are really good at school tests!

Geminis make natural detectives because they are really observant. They are the sign that is best at solving visual puzzles like spot the difference or word searches. Ok, so word searches aren't going to be the next Olympic sport, but being great at puzzles is a fun party trick to show off with and impress your friends!

Cancers are hard workers and very intelligent, which is why they are one of the signs most likely to be earning more than $100,000 a year! Now, just because you're a Cancer doesn't guarantee you're going to see that kind of money without working super hard, but there's something special about this sign that drives them to do well.

Some of the star signs naturally have a lot of energy, and one of these is Leo. Did you know that you're more likely to find a Leo in the gym than any other sign? They love being active, working out, and staying fit.

Obviously, there are billions of people in the world, so plenty of people share the same birthday. But there's one special birthday that is shared by more people than any other, and it happens to be in the star sign of Virgo. What is that special day? It's September 9th.

Which star sign belongs to the most billionaires in the world? According to the Forbes Rich List, it's the sign of Libra. There are currently 32 Libra billionaires in the world; that's 12% of the total number of Billionaires! Will you be one of them when you grow up?

Scorpios have also got a lot to live up to because this star sign has given us more world leaders than any other sign: A total of 22 current and former presidents and prime ministers from different countries have been born under this star sign. Even in the US, there have been more Scorpio Presidents than any other sign.

Do you love performing and dream of being on stage or screen? If you're a Sagittarius, you have a good chance of that dream coming true. If you look back at some of the biggest celebrities who stepped into the limelight as a child, around 20% of them —that's a huge amount!—are Sagittarius. This includes celebrities like Britney Spears and Scarlett Johansson.

If you're a Capricorn, you can feel extra special because you belong to the least common sign. This means that there are fewer Capricorns in the whole world than any other zodiac sign. During the dates ruled by Capricorn, you'll also find the two rarest birthdays, which are December 25th and January 1st.

It's almost as if parents don't want to have to buy too many gifts at the same time!

Are you ready to find out which star sign is yours? Keep reading, and all will be revealed!

CHAPTER 3
HOW TO FIND OUT YOUR ZODIAC SIGN

You probably know when your birthday is, but did you know that your birthday tells you what your star sign is? When you were born, there was a sign of the zodiac that ruled the night sky. Astrologers believe that the particular sign appearing at the moment you were born would influence your personality throughout your life. Over the next chapters, you'll find out all about the signs of the zodiac and how they can make you brave, caring, fun, and creative. First, though, you need to know which sign belongs to you.

• If your birthday falls on or between January 20th and February 18th, then you are an airy Aquarius.

• From February 19th to March 20th, the ruling sign is Pisces, so if your birthday falls on or between those dates, you're one of these sensitive fish.

• Between March 21st and April 19th, Aries is in charge. This fiery ram sign belongs to you if your birthday falls on or between these dates.

• If you celebrate your birthday on or between April 20th and May 20th, then you are under the influence of the earthy Taurus, the great bull.

• Does your birthday fall on or between May 21st and June 20th? If the answer is yes, then the twins of Gemini will be watching over you with their air influence.

• From June 21st to July 22nd, Cancer the crab is in charge. If your birthday falls on or between these dates, then you'll feel at home with this watery sign.

• Between July 23rd and August 22nd is the domain of Leo, the lion, guiding people born on or between these dates with his fiery roar.

• If your birthday falls on or between August 23rd and September 22nd, you are under the earthy influence of Virgo.

• Are you born on or between September 23rd to October 22nd? If so, you are as balanced as your airy zodiac sign, Libra, the scales.

• From October 23rd to November 21st, it is the time of Scorpio the scorpion. This water sign influences anyone who has a birthday on or between these dates.

• Between November 22nd and December 21st, the sign in charge of the skies is Sagittarius, the archer. If you're born on or between these dates, then his fiery arrows will guide your way.

• Finally, if your birthday is on or between December 22nd and January 19th, you are a Capricorn. This mythical half goat, half fish, is the final earth sign on our list.

Now that you know what your zodiac sign is, you can find out all about what that means. Knowing your sign can help you understand why you like some things more than others. It can also help you to know why you find some things easy and others a bit more difficult.

Don't just read your own sign. Knowing the star signs of your friends and family can help you all understand each other better. Have you got a friend who is always quiet and struggles to keep up with you charging around all the time? It sounds like you're a fire sign, and they're a water sign. Instead of energetic activity, they would love to spend time doing something creative with you. Can you and your best friend spend all day playing in a make-believe world? You're probably both air signs who love to daydream and go on adventures in imaginary worlds.

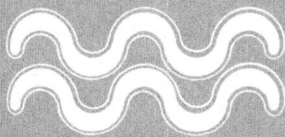

CHAPTER 4
AQUARIUS

Aquarius comes first in this list because it is the star sign that begins its influence in January, but it is actually the 11th sign of the zodiac. It is an air sign and is often shown by a symbol of two horizontal zigzag lines that are meant to show the wind.

The ruling planet for Aquarius is Uranus, the seventh planet from the sun. This cold, blue planet influences the future, which is why Aquarians are so good at planning ahead. It also lends its color to this cool zodiac sign, making light blue an important influence. Lots of people think that Aquarius is a water sign because it is associated with the color blue, but this isn't the case.

Another reason why people wrongly think Aquarius is a water sign is that the constellation of Aquarius, which the star sign is named after, is of a young man carrying a jug of water. This constellation is known as Aquarius, the Water Bearer.

All the signs of the zodiac have their own lucky numbers. They might mean something special to you, or you might get the chance to use them in the future to give yourself some extra luck. For Aquarius, the lucky numbers are 4, 7, 11, 22, and 29.

ALL ABOUT THE AWESOME AQUARIUS!

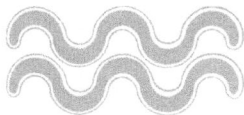

If you are an Aquarius—or you have a friend born under this star sign—you might recognize some of these personality traits. Aquarians like to use their brains a lot. They want to learn new things and have friends that they can talk about them with. This is why they are most happy when working on a group project because they have lots of people to discuss their ideas with.

You can often find an Aquarius deep in thought and trying to solve all the world's problems. However, this does mean that they can get bored quickly if they aren't doing something that challenges them. Aquarians are often drawn to creative subjects like art and music or inventive subjects like science and technology. This is because they can push the boundaries of the subject and come up with new and exciting projects.

Because they like to think a lot, Aquarians are often quiet. You won't often find them charging around and full of physical energy—that kind of behavior is more expected from the fire signs. This quiet quality makes them good listeners, especially if you are telling them your problems. They will be able to help you find solutions and encourage you to think about issues in new ways.

Another good quality that comes from the Aquarius sign is that they want to make everything better. They like to improve the lives of everyone around them. As a grown-up, that could mean creating new inventions or doing charitable work, and as a child, that might mean cutting their neighbor's lawn or helping out with housework. Aquarians like to stand up for what they believe in, which makes them really good at rallying for a cause. An Aquarius would make an awesome class president!

AIRY AQUARIUS ADVENTURES!

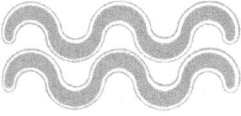

It can take an Aquarius a while to get used to someone, so if you're lucky enough to have one as a friend, make sure you're always kind to them. Aquarius aren't a fan of broken pinky promises or being let down. They take upsets to heart and feel them really deeply. In fact, Aquarians feel all their emotions really strongly, which is great if they're happy and excited about something.

Aquarius people dislike feeling lonely and left out. They love being in a group, but they can also be a little shy about joining in sometimes. The best thing you can do for a friend who is an Aquarius is to invite them to do stuff with you and make sure they always feel included. In return, they'll reward you with interesting conversations, loyalty, and full commitment.

ACQUAINTANCES FOR AQUARIUS!

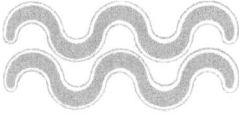

People with the star signs of Libra and Gemini always make good friends with an Aquarius. They are also air signs, and all three tend to think in a similar way. Air signs and fire signs can also make good friends because they can all be quite driven.

Sagittarius also gets on well with Aquarius. The signs are close together on the zodiac wheel, and this means they have a lot in common. Both love to go on adventures and try new things. They also love interesting conversations and activities where they can learn together.

Another good friend for an Aquarius is a Leo. They are opposite signs, but still have a lot in common. They are both loyal to their friends and love spending time in groups. Both these signs care a lot about their friends and will always support them and look after them.

ARTISTIC CAREERS FOR AQUARIUS!

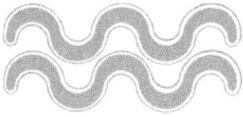

Aquarius signs like to create new things, which is why there are a lot of good Aquarius musicians and actors. If you're feeling shy about standing on the stage, there are plenty of other jobs in the same industry, like making costumes or singing backup vocals in a recording studio.

They're also interested in discovering new things and solving problems, which means that working to develop new technology would keep them fulfilled. Aquarius love to help others, so if that new technology treats diseases or improves society, that's even better. Because Aquarians are so good at explaining things and love to educate others, they often make fantastic teachers.

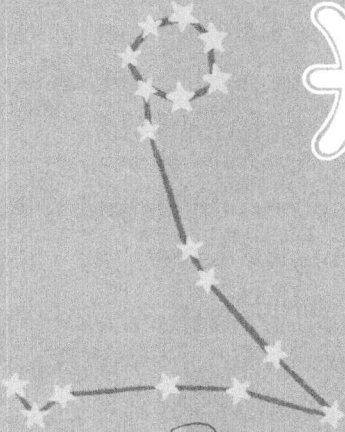

CHAPTER 5
PISCES

Pisces is the 12th and final sign of the zodiac. It takes its name from a constellation of two fish, so it's not surprising that Pisces is a water sign. A special color for Pisces is light green.

Pisces's ruling planet is Neptune, the 8th planet away from the sun. Neptune is called an ice giant because it's big and frosty and covered in icy chemicals, but that doesn't mean Pisces are cold people. In fact, being ruled by Neptune means you have a great imagination and a strong spiritual side.

Like all the other zodiac signs, people born under Pisces have their own set of special numbers that help them in their lives.

You might notice that they keep popping up in things like your phone number, address, or the addresses of your good friends. For a Pisces, the numbers 3, 9, 12, 15, 18, and 24 carry a special meaning.

PRESENTING THE PLEASANT PISCES!

Pisces are big dreamers and will spend their time thinking about mystical and fantastical things. They are extremely open-minded and might get caught up in trying to find answers to the big questions like why is the sky blue, why are flamingos pink, and why do I have to have a bedtime?

If you know a Pisces, they're probably the friend who gives the best emotional support. When you're feeling sad, they'll be there with a shoulder to lean on and an ear to listen to all your problems. Pisces are often called empathetic, which means they are good at sensing other people's emotions and feeling them too. They'll feel happy when you are and sad when you are, which helps to make their friends feel like they're not alone.

Pisces cares a whole lot about their friends' feelings. If you need them, they will make sure to be the best friend they can be and support you. In fact, supporting their friends and family is one of their greatest priorities. If you're a Pisces, then just don't forget to take care of yourself too! But my goodness, aren't your friends and family lucky to have you?

. . .

Like Aquarius, Pisces love to be creative, and if they're not playing music, writing stories, or painting pictures, they might feel like their energy is getting dull. Lots of Pisces choose one of these hobbies to be a big part of their career, either teaching others or performing themselves.

Pisces are very friendly and enjoy meeting new people, which makes it easy for them to make friends. You know you can trust them with your secrets because they're very trustworthy. A Pisces had a big heart with room in it for everyone. They love their friends, their family, and their pets very much.

PISCES PERSONALTIES ARE SO POSITIVE!

Pisces prefer to see the world in a very positive light, where everyone is friends. So, if they see someone being a big meanie, then this can really upset them. Pisces firmly believe in treating others the way you would want to be treated.

Because Pisces are so creative, they can become sad if someone doesn't immediately enjoy their work. A Pisces will pour their heart and soul into their projects, so if someone doesn't quickly show how much they like it, a Pisces might take this to heart. They create art to make others happy, and when this doesn't work, it can make a Pisces very sad.

PALS FOR PISCES!

Pisces are happy to try and get along with everyone, but they will find that some signs make them happier than others. They are drawn to the other water signs, Scorpio and Cancer, but also find it easy to make friends with the earth signs.

Virgo and Pisces work well together because they both want the same thing from a friendship: someone who is always there for them. Both Virgo and Pisces enjoy helping others and being supportive, so by being friends with a Virgo, a Pisces will also have someone looking out for them.

Taurus is another sign that gets on well with Pisces, even though the two signs have opposite characteristics. A Taurus looks at the world in a very realistic way, and a Pisces is more of a dreamer. Together, they work well to balance each other out. They also both enjoy spending time with someone who can show them different ways of thinking.

PROFESSIONS THAT POWER UP A PISCES!

Because Pisces are so caring, a job where they can look after other people would be very fulfilling. From doctors and nurses to childcare and even pet-sitting, there are many different ways a Pisces can spend their time helping others. Pisces also make good therapists because of their ability to relate to how other people are feeling.

Another good option for Pisces is to do something creative and artistic. They love designing and making something new, telling stories, and adding a little more magic back into the world. An ordinary baker might make cakes, but a Pisces baker will decorate wonderful birthday cakes that will steal the show at any birthday party!

CHAPTER 6
ARIES

When the zodiac was created by ancient astrologers, they chose the start date to be the day in springtime when the sun is right above the Earth's equator. This is called the Vernal Equinox, and it's a special day because the length of the day and the night are exactly the same. The zodiac starts on this day with Aries, the first sign of the zodiac.

Aries is a constellation that looks like a huge ram. In Greek mythology, this ram had a rare, golden fleece. Because Aries is a fire sign, its special color is red. Aries is also ruled by the red planet Mars. Mars is the fourth planet from the sun and is thought to make people determined and driven to succeed.

CHAPTER 6

People born with the star sign Aries also have their own set of lucky numbers. These are 1, 8, and 17. It's not really surprising that this includes the number one because Aries love to be first at everything!

48

ALL ABOUT THE AMAZING ARIES!

Aries are full of energy. They always have to be doing something, and they can't stand being bored. Whatever they're doing, Aries strive to be the best because they're very competitive. An Aries will work hard and be really focused on learning everything they can do to improve their game. Aries are particularly good at independent sports, such as tennis, golf, and chess because they are so focused. (However, they also make a great team member!)

Do you have something that you love more than anything else and wish everyone else did too? Aries can be really passionate and enthusiastic, and they love sharing this with others. Once an Aries finds what they enjoy, they throw their heart and soul into it.

They are also really determined and don't like to be stuck on a problem. So, if you're an Aries, make sure to take the time to think of the best fix to the problem and not rush in! This can make all the difference.

Aries are really fun to have as friends because they are always thinking of exciting things for everyone to do. They love meeting new people and will talk to anyone without feeling shy or nervous. Aries never worry about what people think of them because they know they're awesome!

It's clear to everyone that Aries is a fire sign because they have so much energy. This fire also powers their emotions, making their inner feelings very obvious. You won't have to guess what kind of mood they're in!

AN ARIES LOVES TO STAY ACTIVE!

Because Aries are so active all the time, it throws them off if there is a delay or an interruption. Because of their fiery nature, Aries don't do well with boredom. Although these things might create a grumpy Aries, don't worry, they cheer up super quickly!

Aries can also feel frustrated if they don't think they're showing off their best skill. Aries might feel more at home on the sports field, and they would prefer to use their sporting talent than stay indoors. This is an important thing to think about when picking a career. Aries love to do things they're good at and would rather shine by putting their skills to good use.

ALLIES OF AN ARIES!

The other fire signs, Leo and Sagittarius, will always have a good time with an Aries. These signs are all full of the same bright energy, and they love to be active together. Leo and Sagittarius can keep up with an Aries's thoughts and ideas and will give as good as they get in a discussion.

Leo and Aries are almost always going to be best friends. Both signs love adventures and exploring new things, so when they get together, they will never be bored. Aries and Leo are both really good communicators. They will listen to each other's opinions, even if they are different.

Another sign that gets on well with Aries is Libra. They are on opposite sides of the zodiac wheel, and this means that they have opposite personalities, but that also means that they balance each other. Aries love to lead and make decisions, which is exciting for Libra. Libra people are calmer and more gentle, which means they won't argue with Aries and are more likely to agree with them than disagree.

ADVENTUROUS EMPLOYMENT FOR ARIES!

Aries love a challenge and will often want a career where they can rise to the top. Aries make great salespeople because they find it easy to talk to others. Just like teachers give rewards for good grades and behavior, sales jobs often do something similar for doing well called a bonus, and Aries love striving for a prize!

Aries also make great managers. They love to lead teams and inspire people. Lots of jobs in the business world need managers to run teams of workers, so an Aries can always find a management job in an area that they are interested in.

Because Aries are adventurous, they will enjoy a job that takes them to new places. Working as a tour guide or teaching surfing to tourists would be ideal. Not only can they meet lots of interesting people, but they get to show off their local knowledge. They will also have plenty of free time on their days off to go exploring by themselves or with their friends.

CHAPTER 7
TAURUS

The second sign of the Zodiac is another strong animal: Taurus, the bull. Taurus is an earth sign, and its ruling planet is Venus, the second planet from the sun. This combination makes Taurus want to feel connected to everyone and everything. They are very sensory orientated, which means hugs from their dogs and cats and petting animals are sure to make Taurus happy!

Being an earth sign, it's obvious why Taurus's signature color is green, but they also have another special color: pink. They have special numbers, too, and these can bring a Taurus good fortune. Taurus's special numbers are 2, 6, 9, 12, and 24.

THE TERRIFIC TAURUS!

One of the main qualities of an earth sign is that they are solid and dependable. People who are born under the star sign of Taurus are no different. You can rely on a Taurus to always be there for you when you need them. You can also trust them as a study partner because they will definitely deliver their parts of the project.

Taurus are also hard workers. They won't quit until a project has been completely finished, even if that takes many months. If you need someone to help you finish a long video game, then a Taurus is the one to ask. They don't mind if something takes ages because another good quality of a Taurus is that they are very patient.

You won't often find a Taurus daydreaming away with their head in the clouds. Taurus are very down to earth—what else would you expect from an earth sign?—and although they enjoy the creativity of fantastical worlds and ideas, they often prefer to pay attention to the world around them.

Taurus love to be creative and make beautiful things, especially if this includes natural elements. They are very much at home when gardening and looking after colorful flowers, but they might also enjoy cooking, painting, and playing music. Taurus are very practical, so making things—or looking after things—with their hands will bring them joy.

Although fire signs are super quick to make friends, Taurus, on the other hand, like to take their time. When you're friends with a Taurus, it can be a friendship that lasts a lifetime! Taurus are very supportive friends, and they always offer help: For example, if your bike chain breaks, then they will be the first to help you out.

TAURUS TREASURE TIME AND TASKS!

Taurus are sometimes so grounded in the real world that they can't stand when something changes. A sudden change of plans can upset them and make them feel flustered. Luckily, a good pat on the back and a calm word from their friends are often enough to make them feel stable once again.

Taurus like to think things through carefully and usually have their whole day mapped out. This means they usually like things to go to plan and prefer not to have changes in their day.

TEAM UP WITH A TAURUS!

The other earth signs—Virgo and Capricorn—make good friends for a Taurus. This is because they all think in a similar, practical way. Taurus may find it difficult to get on with the more outgoing signs like Leo and Aries or the imaginative Aquarius, who is always dreaming about the future.

Have you ever heard the saying that opposites attract? It's true for magnets, but it's also true for Taurus and their opposite star sign, Scorpio. Instead of annoying each other with their different ways of thinking and behaving, they are brought together by what they have in common. Taurus and Scorpio are both very loyal and supportive people, which is what you need to build a strong friendship. Scorpio can show Taurus how to be energetic and excited about new adventures, and Taurus will teach Scorpio how to make plans and be reliable.

CHAPTER 7

TREMENDOUS TRADES FOR A TAURUS!

There are lots of things about a Taurus that make them really good workers. Any career that needs them to work on projects, make plans, and think about the small details, will keep a Taurus occupied and fulfilled. Taurus are also fantastic at managing their finances, so working in a bank or in the financial industry would be right up their street.

Working in nature is another great avenue for a Taurus. They would love working as a farmer, looking after animals at the zoo, or studying plants as a botanist. Even a job in a florist shop or as a landscape gardener would be interesting to this earthy sign.

CHAPTER 8
GEMINI

This sign is named after two different people from Greek mythology: the twins Castor and Pollux. This is the third sign of the zodiac and another sign associated with the element of air. Gemini is often represented by the color yellow, making it a bright and cheerful sign.

The ruling planet for all Geminis is Mercury, the closest planet to the sun. Mercury was the messenger for the gods, and this planet makes Geminis really good at communicating with others.

All the zodiac signs have special numbers that are considered extra lucky. Gemini's numbers are 5, 7, 14, and 23. If you're a

Gemini and you notice these numbers appearing in your life, it could be a sign that the universe is sending good things your way.

GLANCE AT THE GREAT GEMINI!

Because Gemini is represented by two twins, they have a whole lot of personalities rolled into one person. Sometimes, a Gemini can seem to switch from one behavior to another—like going from really chatty and friendly to suddenly being quiet and needing to be alone. This is perfectly normal, and part of the fun of knowing a Gemini is that they are so adaptable.

Adaptability makes Gemini the least stubborn of all the star signs. They love change and will often look for new experiences. Gemini rarely stand still and like to hang out with lots of groups of friends, doing different activities and projects. It's a good thing that they make friends so easily because they enjoy a lot of different friends to keep them occupied.

Gemini love to talk, and they are happy chatting away with anyone and everyone. You won't find them starting arguments with people who have a different opinion. In fact, a Gemini is most likely to change their mind if you tell them some new facts.

If you have a Gemini friend, then you are truly blessed because they are the most gentle and kind people. They are also fun-loving and will make sure that you always have a good time together. Geminis care a lot about their friends and will show this by showering them with admiration whenever they get the chance.

GEMINI GLEAM IN GROUPS!

Because Geminis are always on the hunt for something new to do, it drives them bananas to do the same thing over and over. If they get stuck in the same routines, they will try to get out of it any way they can. But of course, everyone needs routines like brushing their teeth and doing homework, so Geminis prefer to make it fun!

Geminis don't like being alone. Even though they love things like reading, listening to music, and watching movies, they would much rather do these things with their friends than by themselves. If a Gemini does decide they need to have some alone time, it won't be for very long, and they will soon be back to their social selves.

GETTING ALONG WITH A GEMINI!

It's almost impossible not to get on with a Gemini because they are so outgoing and friendly. Water signs can find this difficult to handle because they want a deeper friendship, but fire signs love the social energy that Gemini have.

But the best signs to get on with a Gemini are the other air signs, Aquarius and Libra. They love to have long, intelligent discussions and come up with new ideas and adventures together.

Because Gemini have two twins looking over them, they can sometimes feel like two different people. They need a good friend who doesn't mind that they're outgoing one day and want to be home alone the next, and Gemini will find this match in a Sagittarius. Sagittarius are easygoing, and they thrive in changing situations, so they'll have no problem managing a Gemini's colorful emotions. They'll also pull Gemini along on their adventures and introduce them to lots of exciting new experiences.

GREAT JOBS FOR A GIFTED GEMINI!

To be really satisfied in their career, Gemini need to have a job where they do something different every day. They tend to get bored working on the same project until it is finished, and they would much prefer engaging in different activities and being in a different environment as much as possible. This is why Gemini flourish in jobs such as photography or tour managing pop stars, where they will visit a new place and meet new people each day!

Other good careers for Geminis involve situations where they have to communicate well with others, like being a teacher or a tutor. Not only is every day different, but Gemini are so friendly and chatty that they will be able to connect with even the most difficult students.

Geminis love to be their own boss, so working as a freelancer or running their own company is a dream job. When a Gemini is in charge of their own career, they can do exactly what they want and pursue their own interests. When they're inspired by what they love, they will work really hard, so it's a win-win situation.

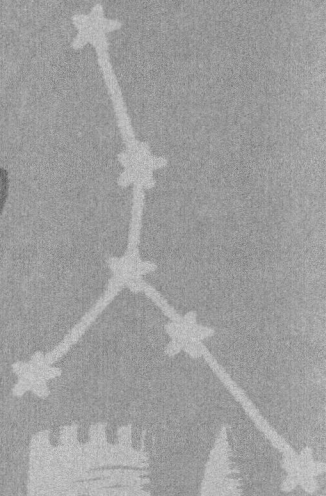

CHAPTER 9
CANCER

The fourth sign of the zodiac is another water sign. This sign is named after the constellation of a giant crab. You might think that the color associated with Cancer would be red—like a crab —but it's actually white. This makes sense when you find out that Cancer is ruled by the moon.

In fact, Cancer is one of only two zodiac signs that doesn't have a ruling planet. The moon isn't a planet, but it is really important to the Earth because it helps to make the tides flow. This makes it really connected to water, so, of course, it is linked to a water sign.

CHAPTER 9

Cancer has its own set of special numbers, just like the other zodiac signs. These are 2, 3, 15, and 20. Keep an eye out, and you might see them pop up in your life as good luck charms.

CHARACTERISTICS OF A CANCER!

Emotions are really important to all the water signs. Cancer signs are known to let their emotions make their decisions for them and are usually guided by what they feel. They are often known to make their choices with their heart: if a Cancer wants ice cream for dinner, that's what they're going to have!

Cancers are very good at sensing the emotions of others, and they will do everything they can to make sure that their friends and family feel loved. These people are very special to Cancer, and they can't feel relaxed and at home if anyone they love is unhappy.

Although Cancers enjoy socializing, they really thrive during their "me time." Because Cancers are so independent during their "me time," they find it a lot easier to stay focused without any distractions. This means they are really good at getting their homework done or finishing a project they are working on, such as a painting or coding an awesome video game!

CANCERS ARE CALM AND CARING!

It can take some time for a Cancer to warm up to new people, but when they do, it becomes a genuine friendship. They are sociable but sometimes a little shy. They value a friend they can confide in, so make sure you keep your pinky promises with a Cancer!

Being around family and hanging out at home is really important to a Cancer because this is their favorite space. They have strong family values and will defend their pack like a true hero! You can always rely on a Cancer to stand by you when you need them the most.

COMPANIONS FOR A CANCER!

Because Cancers are so in tune with their feelings, they need friends who understand their quiet nature. The signs most capable of being kind and gentle with Cancer are the other water signs, Pisces and Scorpio. They know what it feels like to be highly aware of your own emotions and can give Cancer the space and understanding they need to feel valued.

Earth signs Capricorn and Libra also get on well with Cancer because they are stable and grounded. They are both loyal and respect the hard work needed to earn Cancer's trust. Capricorn also shares the same work ethic as Cancer—both signs like to focus completely on their projects—so they make a great team. Libra and Cancer both enjoy a super cozy space wherever they are, so Libra knows how important it is to make an awesome environment for Cancer to relax in.

CREATIVE CAREERS FOR A CANCER!

Cancers know how important it is to have a comfortable space, so a career where they help others to find this would be very rewarding. Whether it's working as a realtor, a decorator, or an interior designer, Cancer will thrive in the emotional reward of seeing their customers satisfied.

Architecture is another great career choice that will let Cancers design the homes of others. Architects tend to work by themselves, and their designs can include a lot of fine detail. Both of these things allow a Cancer to be their most productive.

Being able to sense the emotions of others is a strong Cancer trait, and many often seek a career where they can put this to good use. Cancers make great nurses, nannies, social workers, and home carers. They love looking after others and will treat everyone with the same care and respect.

CHAPTER 10
LEO

This outgoing fire sign is the fifth sign of the zodiac. On the zodiac wheel, Leo appears opposite Aquarius, which tells you that these signs have opposite personalities. Leo is named after the constellation of a great lion that prowls the night sky. This sign's colors are bright and fiery: gold, orange, and yellow.

Leo doesn't have a ruling planet; instead, it has a ruling star! Leo is ruled by the sun. The sun is the brightest part of the solar system, and so Leos like to be the most vibrant part of their family and friendship circles, too. They are full of life, and they light up everyone around them!

Leos should keep an eye out for the following special numbers popping up throughout their life: 1, 3, 10, and 19. If you see one of these, it could be a sign that you're moving in the right direction.

LEARN ABOUT THE LEGENDARY LEO!

The lion is the king of the jungle, and Leos tend to feel like the leader of the pack wherever they go. They love to be center stage and enjoy all that comes with being a star. Leo is never happier than when their talents and personality are on show, whether they're giving a performance or talking in a group.

Leos are great to work with on school projects because they'll take charge and organize everyone. They'll also be more than happy to give the final presentation because they love speaking in front of the class. They get all of their confidence from the ruling sun and can't wait for their chance to shine.

CHAPTER 10

Leos have a kind heart and look after everyone in their pack while making incredible friends. They're always up for fun, energetic, and exciting activities, so you know you will have a good time if there's a Leo in your group.

LEOS LOVE TO LEAD!

Because Leos can come across as very confident, people often forget that they have feelings too. Make sure to treat your Leo friends with the same kindness and compassion that you give to everyone.

Leos are well known for being one of the more willful signs. They know what they want to do and how they want to do it. Getting a Leo to change their mind or to make a compromise takes a lot of negotiating because Leos don't give up easily. This can be a good thing if you've got a problem to solve because Leos will keep working on it until they find the answer!

LINK UP WITH A LEO!

Other fire signs, Aries and Sagittarius, have the same loud and vibrant energy as Leo, so when they all get together, fireworks can happen. This can lead to lots of fun and excitement.

Some signs that make fantastic friends for Leos are the air signs Gemini and Aquarius. Fire needs air to burn, so it totally makes sense that fire and air signs make great friends. The air signs like a challenge, and trying to energetically keep up with a Leo is certainly that.

LIVINGS FOR A LEO!

Leos are great in the limelight, so any career where they can take a starring role is perfect. Being an actor or a politician will bring Leo lots of adoring fans. For those Leos who prefer to be a little more in the background but still want to enjoy the rich and famous lifestyle, there are plenty of careers, such as being a talent agent, personal assistant, or photographer.

Being creative comes naturally to Leos, so they will also enjoy a job where they get to use their arty natures. Being an artist or a designer could be fun for a Leo. They're also not afraid of hard work, so they will happily put in the effort needed to market their work and make a name for themselves.

CHAPTER 11
VIRGO

Virgo is the fifth sign of the zodiac and comes at the time when summer is turning into fall. As an earth sign, Virgos feel very connected to nature and the changes that are happening. Even the constellation Virgo shows the goddess of the harvest holding a stalk of wheat.

Virgo follows Leo, and they have similar special colors, but Virgo's colors are more muted. They are pale yellow, beige, and gray. Virgo's ruling planet is Mercury—the same planet as Gemini. This helps Virgos to communicate well with others.

All the star signs have some numbers that can be lucky for them. These numbers might appear in your life, or you could choose them on a sports jersey or locker combination. The lucky numbers for Virgo are 5, 14, 15, 23, and 32.

VITAL FACTS ABOUT THE VIBRANT VIRGO!

Virgos are absolute perfectionists. Everything they do, right down to the tiniest detail, has to be the best. At school, Virgos make sure that their projects are packed full of great information. They always work hard and enjoy practical tasks like building models and doing science experiments.

They pay the same attention to their friendships. They always remember everyone's birthday, what their favorite snack food is, and who likes what sports. They work hard to make sure that everyone else is enjoying themselves, but this can mean that they don't get a lot of time to do what they want. Virgos aren't good at just doing nothing either, so they find it difficult to relax.

VIRGO

Virgos can be a little hard on themselves when they think they haven't done something to the best of their ability. They need to have good friends around them to remind them of how awesome they are!

VIRGO'S VALUES!

Unlike the chatty fire and air signs, Virgos can be shy around groups of people they don't know well. They would much rather spend time with a small group of good friends than go to a big, loud party.

Virgos are gentle, loving, and caring, and they prefer to be around others that feel the same way. They really don't appreciate it when someone isn't kind, no matter what the circumstances.

VISITORS FOR VIRGO!

Virgos feel most at home when spending time with other earth signs. They share their down-to-earth way of thinking and their love of nature. Virgos also have good friendships with the water signs Cancer and Pisces.

Pisces are happy to let Virgo take their time making friends because they know this will lead to a deep friendship. Cancer and Virgo both have a similar approach to work—they like to get all the details right—so Cancer will understand Virgo's need to take care in everything they do.

VOCATIONS FOR A VIRGO!

Being detail-oriented makes Virgo ideal for careers in science and mathematics. Accountants work with other people's finances and make sure there are no errors in their paperwork—something that a Virgo would love. There are a lot of fine details to be worked on as a researcher, and Virgos make very careful scientists.

Virgos are good communicators, so they would also enjoy working as an editor. It would be their job to make sure that there were no mistakes in books before they were published. They have great attention to detail and wouldn't get bored, even if it took them days to read everything through. They would also enjoy helping to send stories out into the world.

CHAPTER 12
LIBRA

This air sign is the seventh sign of the zodiac. Libra is named after the constellation, which is a picture of a set of scales. This helps Libras to be balanced, and they don't like it when people go to extremes. Libra is ruled by Venus, which also means they are all about finding harmony.

The colors most associated with Libra are pink and green. These colors might not seem like they go well together, but this suits the part of Libra's personality that wants to make peace between different sides.

Libra has a set of special numbers, just like all the other signs of the zodiac. These are 4, 6, 13, 15, and 24. If you are a Libra, keep an eye out to see if these numbers appear in your life. If they do, they might mean you are in for some good luck!

LEARN ABOUT THE LOYAL LIBRA!

Libras often feel like it's their duty to solve all the world's problems, and they don't like anything that isn't fair. Libras are very good at deciding how to share things equally and finding solutions to problems that suit everyone. If you're working in a group, you can rely on the Libras to make sure that each person does their fair share of the work and gets equal praise at the end.

Like other air signs, Libras don't like to fight. They are very peaceful people and stay out of arguments as much as possible. However, it's not possible to make everyone happy at the same time, even though Libras always try their very best. They like talking to others and are at ease in groups of people.

As you would expect from a sign that doesn't like conflict, Libras are very gentle and caring. They will go out of their way to make sure that they never upset their friends. Libras are great at talking through their problems and letting everyone know how they are feeling, and they can also inspire others to do the same. Once they've got everybody talking, they can use their diplomatic skills to settle any problems.

Because Libras don't like to say or do anything that will upset anyone, they will often wait to see what others will say or do before offering their own opinion. This is extremely considerate. However, if you're a Libra, don't forget that your opinion matters too, and sometimes it's worth speaking up!

LIBRAS WILL LIFT YOUR SPIRIT AND LISTEN!

Libras are all about balance, so they can't stand to see any injustice and will jump in to help whenever possible. They get really upset if they see things like bullying or inequality. This could be in their own friendship group, in school, or in the wider world. When a Libra spots something out of harmony, they will do whatever they can to make things right, even if they didn't cause the problem.

Libras can't stand mess! They really appreciate and take care of their things, like clothing, technology, toys, and furniture. This is great news for parents, as a Libra will keep their room tidy without having to be told twice!

LIFE LONG FRIENDS FOR LIBRA!

The air signs—Aquarius, Gemini, and, of course, other Libras—will understand Libra the best, and these make for life-long friends. They will respect Libra's commitment to justice and not pull them into arguments for fun.

Surprisingly, Libra can get on very well with Aries and Sagittarius, despite them being fire signs. They understand Libra's passion for harmony. Aries is the opposite sign to Libra, meaning they're on different sides of the zodiac wheel. Opposites can work really well together as friends because they balance out each other's behaviors. Libra can calm down Aries and help them to see the other side in a disagreement. Aries can inspire Libra to become more self-assured and stand up for themselves!

LINES OF WORK FOR A LIBRA!

Because Libras are committed to fighting injustice and restoring harmony, they like to choose careers where they can make a real difference. Working as a lawyer is an obvious choice, but if that doesn't sound like fun, there are other jobs working with the law that will also satisfy a Libra. Legal secretary, clerk, and judge might also appeal to Libra's sense of justice.

Because of a Libra's goal of restoring harmony on the planet, they may pick a career that will help the environment, such as an environmental or conservation scientist!

A counselor or psychiatrist is another good choice. Both jobs involve helping others to talk through their problems, and this means Libra can use their excellent communication skills. Whether they're helping people to solve an inner conflict or a disagreement with another person, Libra will feel happy knowing that they have helped to bring a little more harmony into the world.

SCORPIO

CHAPTER 13
SCORPIO

Scorpio is the eighth sign of the zodiac, and it belongs to the group of star signs called the water signs. This is strange because scorpions—the animal that Scorpio is named after—live in the desert, where there is very little water. Scorpio's influential colors reflect this because they're not watery colors at all: they are scarlet, red, and rusty orange.

The ruling planet for Scorpio is the planet Pluto—even though it is no longer called a planet by NASA, it can still have an influence on our lives. Pluto is all about change and transformation, and Scorpios often have multiple layers to their feelings and their personality.

There are some special numbers that Scorpios might like to keep in mind. These numbers can be lucky for you or might help you make the right choice if they pop up in certain situations. These special numbers are 8, 11, 18, and 22.

SAY HELLO TO THE SENSATIONAL SCORPIO!

Like the other water signs, a Scorpio is very in tune with their emotions. It might not seem like they are, though, because they are very good at looking calm on the surface when they might actually be a little bit upset. Being able to stay calm, even when everything is going wrong, is something that makes Scorpios natural leaders!

Scorpios love to be successful in everything that they do. Once they know what they want, they are really focused on getting it. They're great to work with because you know that they won't avoid their responsibilities. It's not just hard work that makes Scorpios successful: They're very charismatic, fun, and incredible at making friends!

Just like the scorpion, Scorpios aren't afraid to take on big challenges. They are very brave and will always stand up for what they believe in. You can count on Scorpios to make positive changes in the world!

SCORPIO'S ARE STAND UP SIGNS!

Once a Scorpio trusts you, they'll open up and share a whole new side that you didn't know they had. Being trusted by a Scorpio is a true privilege, so make sure they can count on you.

Standing up for their beliefs is a core Scorpio trait, and when they believe they are right about something, they will stick by it! However, if you offer a different perspective, then a Scorpio will always hear you out.

SIDEKICKS FOR SCORPIO!

Scorpios get along the best with water signs because they understand their emotional qualities the best. Cancer is especially good with Scorpio because they can sense their hidden emotions and know just what to say to calm them down and help them settle.

Another sign that gets on well with Scorpio is Taurus. This grounded earth sign isn't easily flustered by Scorpio, and in return, Scorpio appreciates the reliability and predictability of a Taurus friend.

SUCCESSFUL PROFESSIONS FOR SCORPIO!

Scorpios will work hard at whatever task they are given, but they really like projects that they can dedicate their time to. They love digging into the finer details, so a job as a researcher is ideal. Working alone suits a Scorpio, and they will enjoy showing others their findings and sharing their incredible knowledge on a subject.

Another good job would be working as an engineer. This career allows Scorpio to spend all day fixing problems. They will also enjoy seeing the real-world benefits of their work, and engineering projects often result in a new machine, building, or infrastructure.

Any career path that gives a Scorpio a chance to challenge themselves is going to appeal to them. They enjoy success and being the best that they can be, no matter how much hard work it takes. Something like a detective or a surgeon, where their commitment and their strengths will be recognized, would be an ideal choice.

CHAPTER 14
SAGITTARIUS

This energetic fire sign is the ninth sign of the zodiac and is ruled by the king of the planets, Jupiter, the fifth planet from the sun. This planet is all about positive vibes, bringing luck, hope, prosperity, and growth to those under its influence. Sagittarius influences some of the darkest months of the year, and to make up for the lack of light, this star sign creates some of the most bright and uplifting people.

Despite being a fire sign, the influential color for Sagittarius is blue. This might be a link to their traditional role as a healer: Sagittarius's constellation is the centaur Chiron, who was a great teacher and healer in Greek mythology.

CHAPTER 14

Sagittarius has a set of special numbers that can have a strong influence on the lives of people born under this sign. These numbers are 3, 7, 9, 12, and 21. If you're a Sagittarius, you might notice these numbers appearing in your life to show you that you're on the right path.

STARRING THE SINCERE SAGITTARIUS!

Following the intense Scorpio, Sagittarius is the exact opposite. People born under this sign are eternal optimists, always seeing the best in people and situations. They expect everyone to be as good and kind as they are and are always open and honest about these expectations.

Sagittarius love people. They always want to find out new things about different cultures and different places, and the best way to do this is to talk to people who have lived there. A Sagittarius's friendship group will be large and filled with all sorts of different people rather than just those who are like them. They are more than happy to spend time with people they have nothing in common with: Sagittarius sees this as an opportunity to try something new rather than writing off a friendship straight away.

Because Sagittarius is always trying to learn or do something new, they can get frustrated when stuck in the same routine. They love to learn new things and are really good at researching and teaching themselves. You might also find that they offer interesting new perspectives that you hadn't thought of before.

SAGITTARIUS'S ARE SELF-SUFFICIENT!

Sagittarius love to be free to follow their own path and set their own boundaries; they really do march to the beat of their own drum. They take their friends on the best adventures, often taking them places that they've never been!

Part of being such an open and honest sign is that Sagittarius people are never afraid to say what they mean. They don't get upset too easily, but of course, they would like to have their opinions valued and not overlooked. Even if a Sagittarius accidentally said something that upset someone else, then they likely didn't mean it to come off that way because they are loving and helpful.

SOCIALIZING WITH A SAGITTARIUS!

Aries makes an excellent friend for Sagittarius because they have many things in common. Both are fire signs, meaning that they are full of energy and love doing exciting and adventurous things. They both love to try new activities, so visiting a new trampoline park in town or eating at a new pizza place would be the perfect time for this adventurous duo!

Gemini also get on well with Sagittarius. They don't like being still and can't wait to try new things. Together, Gemini and Sagittarius will push each other to find new hobbies and activities that will keep them from ever getting bored.

Sagittarius might not quickly relate to the water and earth signs and their attachment to their homes. Why stay still when there is the whole world waiting to be explored? If you know someone who finds it hard to sit still and always seems to be trying something new, it's very likely they're a Sagittarius!

SUPERIOR WORK PLACES FOR SAGITTARIUS!

Sagittarius are fun-loving adventure seekers and would be happy in any job that lets them indulge this side of their personality. The travel and hospitality industry is a great starting point. Sagittarius would love working as a travel agent, where they can help others to design their perfect holiday. This will also give them the insider track on some great travel deals for their own vacations!

The creative side of a Sagittarius can be a huge asset at work, and a career as a freelance artist, designer, or architect could be just what they need to showcase their unique style. Bold and adventurous designs won't scare a Sagittarius, and they will enjoy the freedom of working on their own projects as their own boss.

CHAPTER 14

A repetitive 9-5 job will likely stifle the Sagittarius's enthusiasm, so they might prefer to find a job that has some variety. Being a teacher fits the bill perfectly. Every day is always different, and Sagittarius will get to use their excellent communication skills to inspire the children in their class.

CHAPTER 15
CAPRICORN

Capricorn is the tenth sign of the zodiac and the one that starts the latest in the year: on December 22nd. This sign is represented by the constellation Capricorn the Sea Goat—a mythical creature that has the head and hooves of a goat but the tail of a fish, a bit like a mermaid!

Despite living in the sea, Capricorn is an earth sign. To show this, the sign is associated with neutral, earthy colors, including brown and black. The ruling planet for Capricorn is Saturn, the largest planet in our solar system and the sixth planet from the sun. Saturn is the planet of responsibility, strength, and discipline: All qualities that you will find in a Capricorn.

CHAPTER 15

Just like all the other star signs, Capricorn has their own set of lucky numbers. These are 4, 8, 13, and 22. These numbers can help you in your life by guiding you to make the right decisions, so watch out for them.

CELEBRATE THE COOL CAPRICORN!

Capricorns are the opposite of their zodiac neighbors Sagittarius. They love structure and having everything set out in order. If you give a Capricorn clear instructions, they will follow them absolutely, making them excellent study buddies and work partners. They are also very disciplined and can stay focused on the same task for a long time.

Being an earth sign means that Capricorns are very grounded in reality. They often prefer quieter hobbies like reading rather than active hobbies like sports but not always.

Capricorns give their friends the same focus they would give to their work, which makes them excellent pals. Their reliability is one of their best qualities, so they will be sure not to miss a birthday, soccer game, or anything that means a lot to you.

CAPRICORNS CHERISH TRADITIONS!

Capricorns really value their boundaries and don't like to change the familiar ways they do things. They often worry that change won't be good, so it's really important to remind your Capricorn friends (or yourself) that change can be really cool! Imagine a world where you didn't discover your favorite cereal or cartoon because you didn't want to try something new!

Because Capricorns aren't a fan of change, traditions mean a lot to them. This makes them very close to their families, and they really enjoy reliving the memories that traditions bring. They love to remember things like seasonal holidays and family vacations and will be the ones taking lots of photos! So, something like the pizza place their family takes them to every birthday means the world to them, and they look forward to these things every year.

COMRADES FOR CAPRICORN!

Capricorns get on well with all the earth signs, but especially with Taurus. They share a mutual love of being practical and are both hard workers. Taurus lives in the present while Capricorn lives in the past, but these two views work well together, with Taurus encouraging Capricorn to appreciate today.

The air signs—who are always planning for the future—and the fire signs—who are always in search of fun—might find it difficult to be on the same calm level as a Capricorn. Although they might make interesting friends, Capricorns usually prefer to engage in more familiar and peaceful activities at home. One sign that shares a similar enjoyment of home comforts is the water sign, Cancer. Capricorn and Cancer will enjoy a relaxed friendship where they can stay in with a good movie and some popcorn.

CAREERS FOR A COMMITTED CAPRICORN!

Capricorns love to work and can often find it difficult to stop! Finding the balance between their studies or their career, and their friends and family is difficult for this dedicated and driven earth sign. They also want a career with a clear role where they know exactly what is expected of them.

A high school teacher would be the perfect job for a hard-working Capricorn. They love the planning and organization involved and are patient enough to deal with the difficult behavior of some teenagers. The long school holidays also force Capricorn to take a much-needed break and enjoy some relaxing hobbies and hanging out with friends.

Another career that is well-suited to Capricorns is that of a realtor. Hard work is vital in this business if you want to be a success, and Capricorns definitely have enough drive and determination to be great! There's also the chance to manage your own workload, and most realtors work alone or in small teams, which suits a Capricorn completely.

A ZODIAC STONE FOR EACH STAR SIGN!

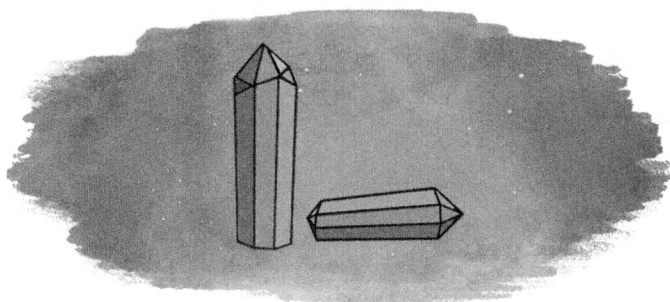

Did you know that each astrological sign has a special mineral or gemstone that is linked with it? Most people know about birthstones, but zodiac stones are a little more specific. Some people like to wear these precious gems to bring good luck, and others just like to keep them around as decoration or in a special box or pouch. Want to know your zodiac stone?

A ZODIAC STONE FOR AQUARIUS: AMETHYST

Amethyst comes in varying shades of purple and violet. One of the countries that produces the most amethyst is Brazil. If you treat amethyst with heat (this means heating it up), it can actually resemble a stone called Citrine. Some people find this stone helps promote calmness and creates clarity in making decisions.

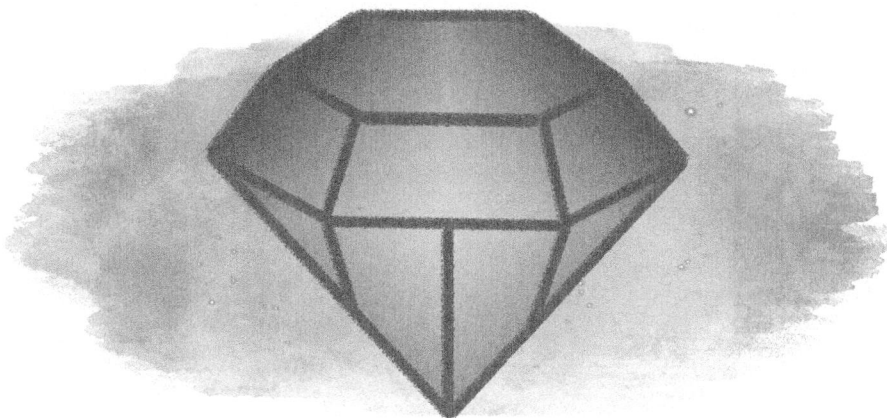

A ZODIAC STONE FOR PISCES: AQUAMARINE

This stone gets its name from the Latin words "Aqua" and "Marina," which translates to "Water" and "Of the Sea." It's no wonder why they named this stone after water and the sea; its colors range from shades of blues and greens that blend together. Some people find this stone empowering and helpful with clear communication!

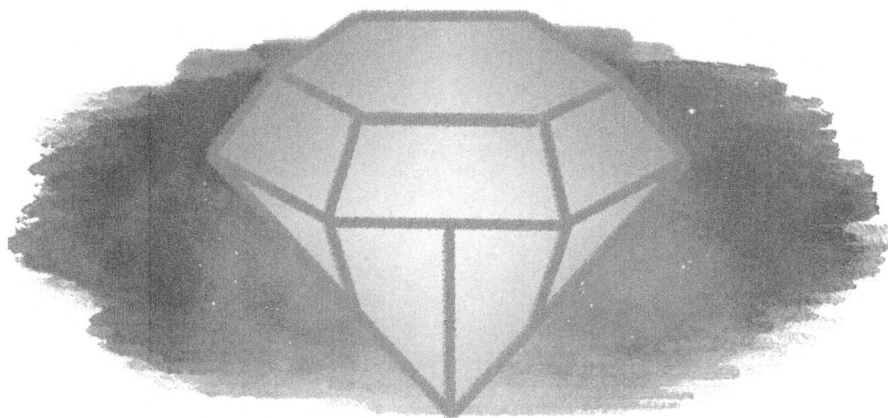

A ZODIAC STONE FOR ARIES: DIAMOND

Diamonds are made of pure carbon, meaning they are the only gem on the planet made of just one element! Although the most common diamond is translucent (clear), they come in a variety of colors like yellow, pink, blue, and many more. The diamond is one of the four main precious stones on earth. Some people believe this stone promotes powerful inner strength.

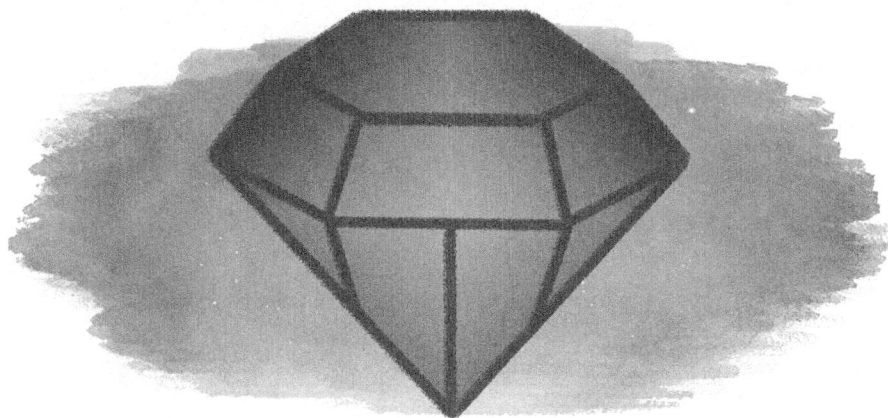

A ZODIAC STONE FOR TAURUS: EMERALD

The emerald is one of the oldest and most sought out stones in history; In fact, it was Queen Cleopatra's (Queen of ancient Egypt) favorite! Its color is a deep vibrant green. The emerald is one of the four main precious stones on earth. Some people believe this stone promotes prosperity (well-being), wealth, and a sense of peace.

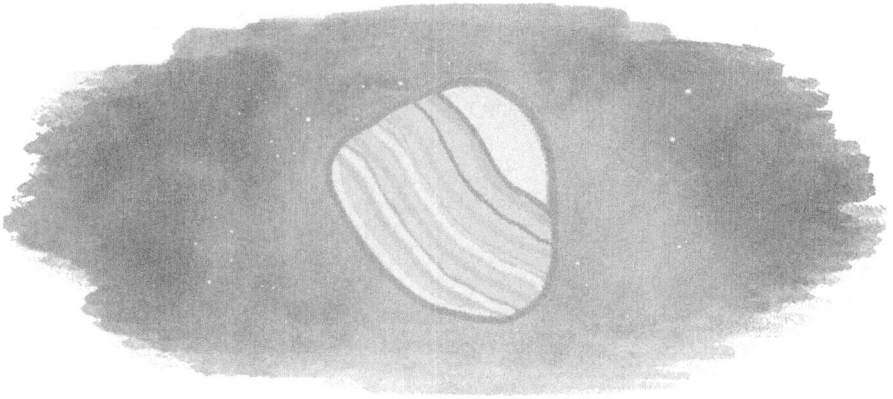

A ZODIAC STONE FOR GEMINI: AGATE

There are so many types of agate, from blue lace agate (blue), moss agate (green), and fire agate (red). These stones vary in color but share a resemblance because of the unique banding (stripes). These stones are a type of quartz called Chalcedony. Some people believe this stone promotes inner stability and raises consciousness.

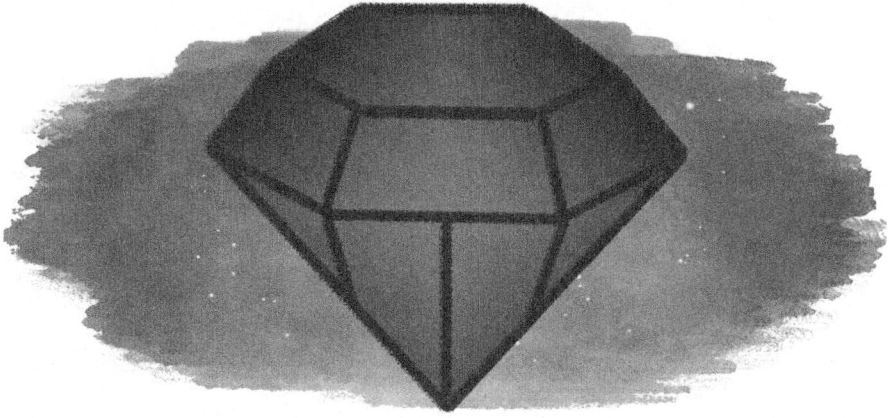

A ZODIAC STONE FOR CANCER: RUBY

The ruby gets its name from the Latin word "rubens," which translates to "red." They are mostly known for being red but can also come in a shade of pink. The ruby is one of the four main precious stones on earth. Some people believe this stone promotes confidence and balance.

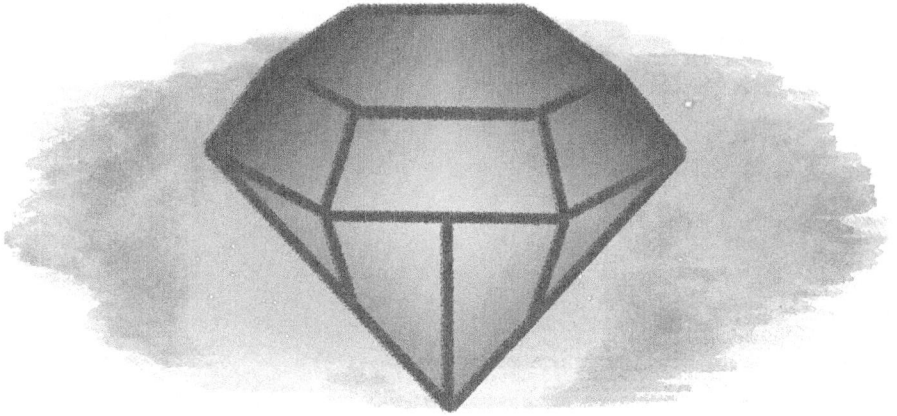

A ZODIAC STONE FOR LEO: PERIDOT

Peridot is one of the only stones that comes in one color, which is green. It is also one of the few stones to be reported outside of earth and found in some meteorites! Some people believe this stone promotes compassion and good fortune!

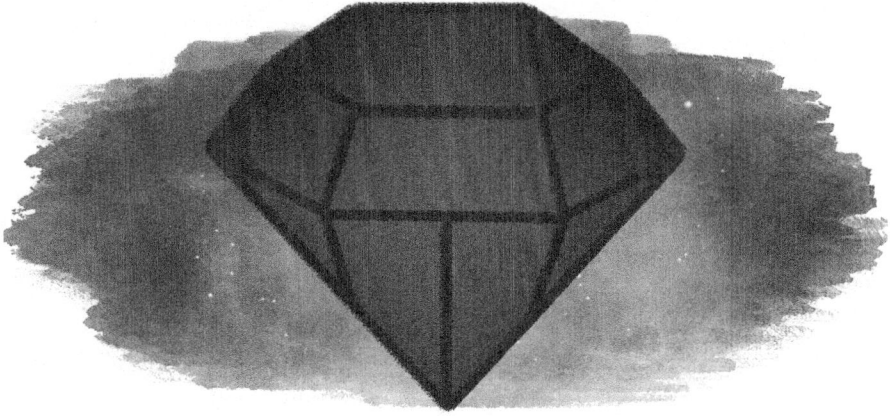

A ZODIAC STONE FOR VIRGO: BLUE SAPPHIRE

Sapphire's color is a deep vibrant blue. Sapphire's name derives from the Greek word "sappheiros," which translates to "blue Stone." The sapphire is one of the four main precious stones on earth. Some people believe this stone promotes self-expression and empathy!

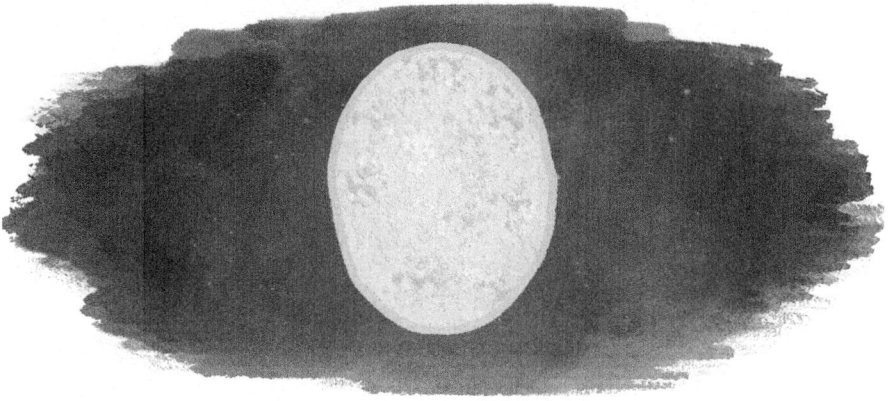

A ZODIAC STONE FOR LIBRA: OPAL

Opal's name derives from the Latin word "opalus," which translates to "precious stone." It is said that about 95% of opal comes from Australia. The color of opal can be described as a milky white or translucent color with shimmer speckles of the rainbow. Some people believe this stone promotes harmony and hope!

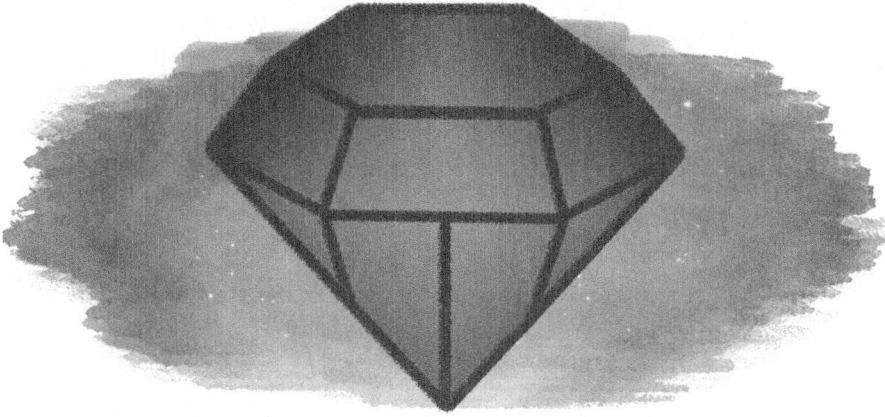

A ZODIAC STONE FOR SCORPIO: TOPAZ

A pure topaz is colorless, so it can often be mistaken for a diamond. They come in many shades of the rainbow, like red, blue, pink, yellow, and green! Red being the most rare, and blue being the most common. Some people believe this stone promotes joy and enthusiasm!

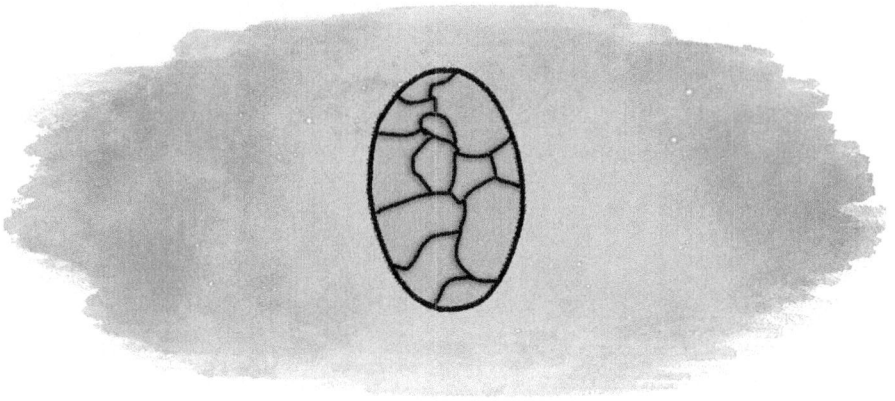

A ZODIAC STONE FOR SAGITTARIUS: TURQUOISE

Turquoise is the only gemstone in the world to have a color named after it. Turquoise's name derives from the French word "turquoise," which translates to "Turkish." Some people find this stone promotes good luck and protection!

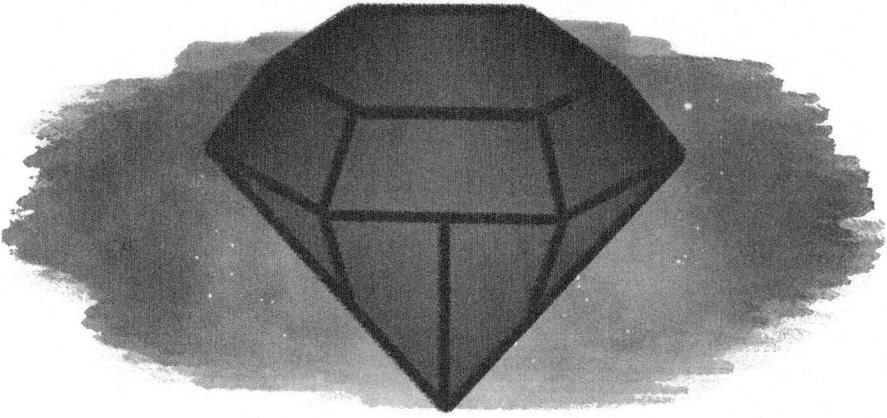

A ZODIAC STONE FOR CAPRICORN: GARNET

Garnet's name comes from the Greek word "granatum," which translates to seed or grain because it resembles the shape and color of a pomegranate seed. Most of the time, garnet is described as a red color, but it actually comes in many different colors, such as green, pink, or gold! Some people find this stone helps promote confidence and boosts their self-esteem!

CONCLUSION!

CONCLUSION!

Have you found it interesting learning about the star signs? I bet you know a lot more now than you did at the start. You're now one of the millions of people, all through the ages, who have started to unlock the secrets of the stars. Next time someone asks you what your star sign is, you can give them a confident answer!

Now that you know all about your star sign, you might understand yourself a lot better. Are you a workaholic Capricorn or a daydreaming Aquarius? Maybe you're a fun-loving Leo or a Cancer who loves curling up at home. Knowing your star sign can help you to see how unique you and your friends are. If they love to speak to everyone, but you feel a little shyer than them, it could be because of the stars above!

What's exciting is that everything you've just learned is only the beginning. There's a lot more to astrology than will fit into one book. If you are interested in investigating further, there are lots more things you can learn.

One thing people love about knowing their star signs is that they can read their horoscope. A horoscope is a prediction of what is going to happen. You can get them for the day or for the whole year. They're often very general and are up to you to work out how they apply to your life, but it can be fun to read that you're going to have a great day!

CONCLUSION!

Not everyone you meet will believe in astrology, and that's ok. Nothing about astrology is a fact; rather, it's supposed to be a guide. Not everything about your sign will fit exactly with who you are, but some parts might be very accurate. Whether you want to use astrology as a bit of fun or you want to look into it in more detail is up to you. It's always good to learn something new, and now you know all about how astrology started and what the different star signs mean!

Have fun on your astrology adventure! Thank you for reading!

CONSTELLATIONS FOR KIDS

THE FUN WAY TO LEARN ABOUT THE STARS, DISCOVER THE MAGIC OF THE SOLAR SYSTEM, AND STARGAZE LIKE AN ASTRONOMER!

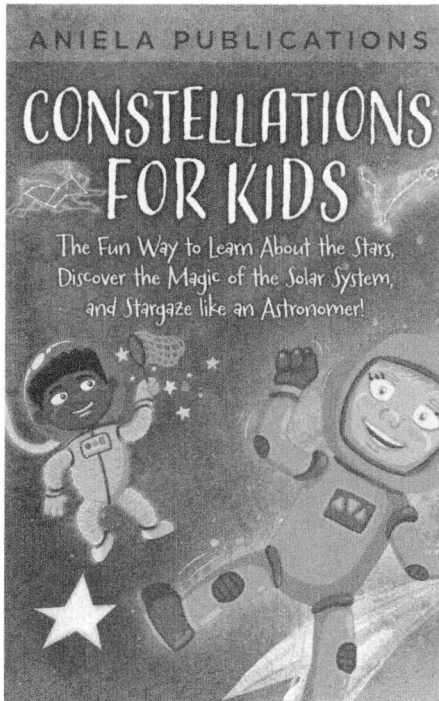

CHAPTER 1
WELCOME TO THE AMAZING WORLD OF CONSTELLATIONS!

CHAPTER 1

Have you ever looked up at the night sky and imagined what might be out there? You're not alone! People have been wondering that for thousands of years. Technology like telescopes and space shuttles are quite new, so before we could really investigate space, people would make up stories about what they thought was up there.

Some people saw heroes and monsters made out of stars and would tell stories about them. We can see those same pictures today because nothing in space changes very quickly. This book is going to tell you all about the wonderful things floating around above your head and teach you how to find some of the planets and special stars from your bedroom window.

THE AMAZING UNIVERSE

The universe is a really big place. It has to be because everything that exists is inside of it! Our planet Earth is only one very tiny part of it. The universe includes the whole of space with all the stars, moons, and planets, and we can only see the ones that are closest to us. Did you know that the universe is still getting bigger? It is growing so quickly that no one will ever be able to get to the edge.

Inside the universe are billions of galaxies made up of stars, dust, and planets. There are more stars in the universe than anything else. Did you know there are more stars than grains of sand on all the beaches on Earth? Stars have fascinated people for thousands of years. The Ancient Greeks used to believe that if you wished on a shooting star, your wish would come true. Have you ever wished on a star?

WHAT IS A CONSTELLATION?

A constellation is a group of stars that form a pattern. Astronomers used imaginary lines to join stars together into shapes, people, and animals. Often these constellations were named after characters in stories like Hercules, Pegasus, and Orion. You might not have heard of them, but they were very famous to the Ancient Greeks and Romans. The largest constellation is called Hydra and looks like a long sea serpent swimming through the sky.

. . .

There are 88 official constellations, and they can be seen from all around the world. Some constellations have smaller patterns inside them called asterisms. The most famous asterism is the Big Dipper which is part of a constellation called Ursa Major.

CONSTELLATIONS IN DIFFERENT CULTURES

Did you know that explorers have found cave paintings showing pictures in the stars? This shows that even cavemen were using their imaginations when thinking about space and what they could see up there. What is really amazing is that people from different countries looked at the stars and saw very similar patterns.

There is a constellation that the Ancient Greeks called Orion. They made up a story about him chasing seven sisters. All the way over in Australia, the Aboriginal people saw the same stars and also told a story about a man chasing seven sisters, but they called him Baiame.

CHAPTER 2
DID YOU KNOW THE STARS LOOK DIFFERENT FROM DIFFERENT COUNTRIES?

If you stand in front of your house, you will see one view of the front door and porch, and if you stand in the back, you will see another view of the back of the house. It's the same with stars.

Because the Earth is round, it is impossible for people on different sides of it to see the same stars at the same time. There are some stars you can see from Canada that will never be seen from Australia.

A LINE ROUND THE MIDDLE OF THE EARTH

The Earth is split into two halves by an imaginary line around its middle. This line is a bit like a belt, and it is called the equator. All the countries and oceans above the equator are in the northern hemisphere. All the countries and oceans below it are in the southern hemisphere.

The northern hemisphere and southern hemisphere never swap over. One is always on the top, and the other is always on the bottom. The constellations mentioned in this book can all be seen from the northern hemisphere.

HOLD ON TIGHT—THE EARTH IS SPINNING!

The Earth also has an imaginary line called an axis going straight through the middle. Imagine sticking a pencil through an orange. That's what the Earth's axis would look like if we could see it! At the top is the North Pole, and at the bottom is the South Pole.

. . .

This axis is important because the Earth turns around it. This is how we get night and day. It's daytime when your country is facing the sun and nighttime when it is turned away from the sun. As the Earth spins around, you can see different stars, and the constellations will appear in different places in the sky. Knowing where they should be at each time of the year is what helped explorers find their way.

WHAT ELSE IS IN OUR SOLAR SYSTEM?

THE SUN

The sun is our closest star, but it is still 147 million kilometers away. It provides us with all our light and heat, and if we didn't have the sun, then we wouldn't be able to survive. It might look quite small up in the sky, but the sun is actually so huge that you could fit one million copies of the Earth inside it!

. . .

We've already said that the Earth spins around its axis, but did you know the Earth also spins around the sun? The path that it takes is called an orbit, and the Earth takes one year to go all the way around the sun and get back to where it started. The Earth's orbit isn't a perfect circle; sometimes, it is closer to the sun, and sometimes it is a little further away. This is why we get summer and winter seasons and why the temperature on Earth changes.

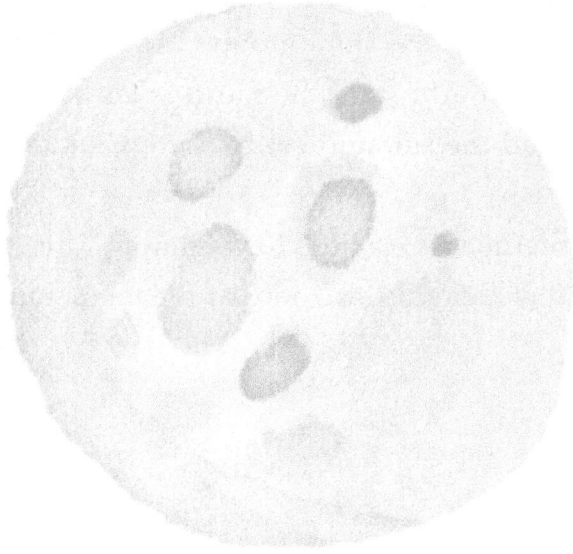

THE MOON

The moon orbits the Earth just like the Earth orbits the sun. It takes 28 days for the moon to go all the way around the Earth. Our moon is one out of more than 200 moons in our solar system. Some other planets have more than one moon. Jupiter, the largest planet, has 80 moons!

You can see the moon at night, but it doesn't give out its own light like the stars do. Instead, we can see the moon because the light from the sun shines on it, and the moon reflects this light down to Earth. Over a month, the moon appears to change shape from a full moon to a crescent moon and back again, but that's actually the shadow from the Earth getting in the way of the sun's light.

The moon is about 384,400 kilometers away from Earth, which doesn't sound very close, but it is actually close enough for us to feel the moon's gravity. The moon's gravity pulls things towards it. It isn't strong enough to move the whole planet Earth, but it does make waves on the ocean and pull the tides in and out.

THE PLANETS

There are eight planets in our solar system, and they all orbit around the same sun. The closest planet to the sun is called Mercury. Next is Venus, then Earth, Mars, Jupiter, Saturn, Uranus, and Neptune. All planets are named after Roman gods except for ours. Some of the planets are made out of rock, like Earth, and others are balls of gas.

Like the moon, light reflects off the planets, and you can see some of them from Earth, even without a telescope! The planets that we can see are Mercury, Venus, Mars, Jupiter, and Saturn.

SHOOTING STARS

Seeing a shooting star can be really exciting. Ancient people used to think they were signs that the gods were listening to their prayers. Thanks to scientists investigating, we now know that shooting stars aren't stars at all. They are actually meteors which are small pieces of dust or rock. When they touch the Earth's atmosphere, they heat up and start to glow. Sometimes you can see meteor showers that can last for days or weeks, and there will be thousands of shooting stars in the sky. The best shower is called the Perseids (pronounced per-see-ids), and it happens every August. You can see a meteor every minute!

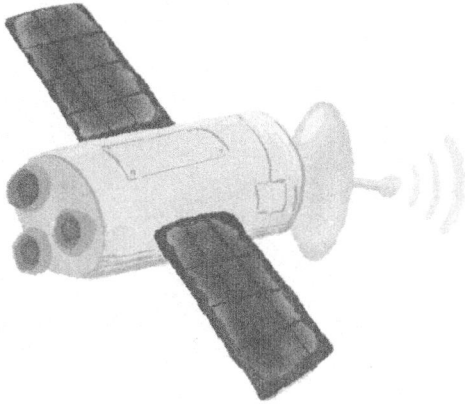

SATELLITES

Not everything in space is natural. There are loads of things that humans have sent up there. If you see a slowly moving star in the sky, it is probably a satellite. Satellites are electronic machines that orbit around the Earth. We use them to send messages around the world, take pictures of the Earth, and check on the weather.

Have your parents got a GPS system in the car or on their phones? There are more than 30 satellites that are used to help people navigate the roads. So next time you see yourself moving on a map, you'll know it's a message sent all the way from space!

CHAPTER 3
OUR GALAXY, THE MILKY WAY

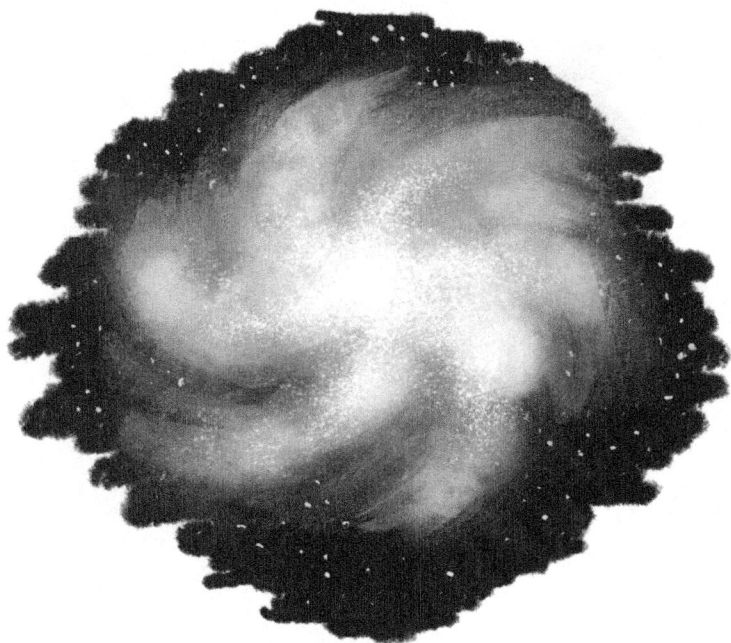

CHAPTER 3

Our solar system is part of a galaxy called the Milky Way. Do you know how it got its name? Roman astronomers looked at the sky and saw a white streak that looked like someone had spilled milk on the stars, so they called it the Milky Way. The Milky Way is home to hundreds of billions of stars and their planets. Everything you can see in the sky is part of our galaxy. There are billions of galaxies in the universe, but ours is the only one that shares its name with a chocolate bar!

STARGAZING AND THE SOLAR SYSTEM: MARVEL AT THE NIGHT SKY!

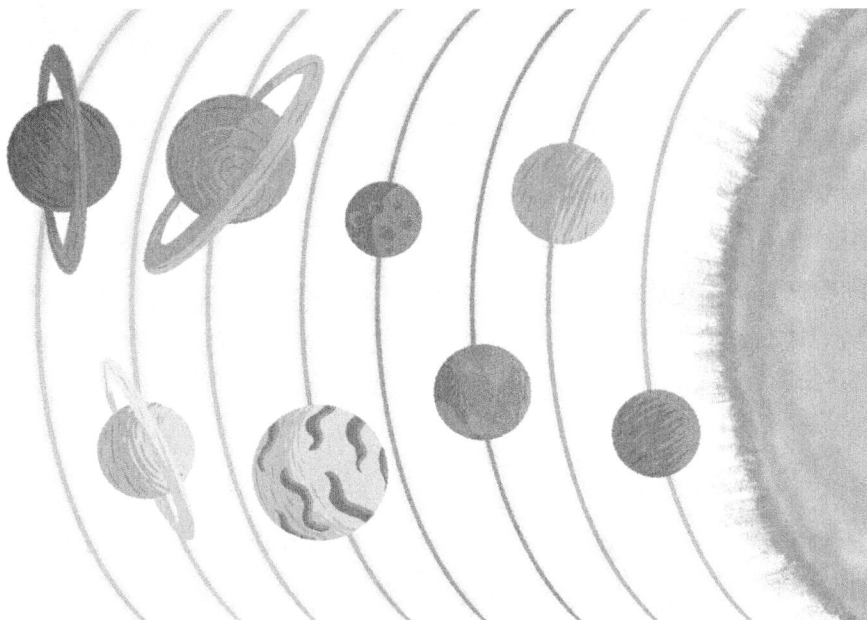

WELCOME TO THE SOLAR SYSTEM

Our solar system is everything that orbits our sun and all the stars, comets, and asteroids that are held in place by its gravity. It's called the solar system because "sol" is an old word for "sun."

MEET THE PLANETS

Mercury is the closest planet to the sun. It is also the smallest planet in the solar system—about one-third as big as Earth.

Days on Mercury are very, very hot, but the nights there are extremely cold. Mercury doesn't have any moons, but it does look a lot like our moon because its surface is covered with craters.

Venus is the second planet from the sun. It spins on its axis really slowly, which means that one day on Venus lasts as long as 243 days on Earth. That's nearly 6,000 hours! The surface of Venus is covered with inactive volcanoes, and its sky is full of yellow clouds.

Earth is the only planet in our solar system that has anything living on it. The other planets are either too hot or too cold. Scientists have spent years looking for signs of life on other planets, but they haven't found anything yet. Aliens must be very good at hide-and-seek!

Mars is known as the "red planet" because it is covered in rusty iron dust. It has volcanoes like Venus, but they are inactive and don't work anymore. Mars has two moons called Phobos and Deimos. There may not be any aliens on Mars, but there are a lot of robots! This is because scientists have been sending them to investigate Mars since 1965.

· · ·

Jupiter is the largest planet in our solar system. It is sometimes called a gas giant because it is almost entirely made of gas. The surface is very windy and full of storms. One of these storms makes a swirling red spot that looks like the planet's eye. It makes Jupiter one of the most easily recognizable planets.

Saturn—another gas giant—has the most moons out of all the planets in our solar system: 82! It is also surrounded by rings made up of rocks and ice. These rings are very beautiful and make Saturn the most unique planet to look at. You can see Saturn's rings from Earth if you use a telescope.

Uranus also has rings, but they are much thinner and less bright than Saturn's. Uranus is an ice giant because it is so cold that some of the gasses in its atmosphere have frozen. Uranus is the only planet that spins on its side. Scientists think this is because it was hit by another planet and knocked over!

Neptune is the furthest planet in our solar system and another ice giant. It is a bright shade of blue because of the types of gases in its atmosphere. Neptune is so far away that only one spacecraft has managed to reach it. This distance makes it difficult for us to know as much about Neptune as we do about closer planets. This means there are still lots of things for scientists to discover.

NO TELESCOPE? NO PROBLEM!

There are lots of things you can see in the night sky without any special equipment. In fact, the first astronomers didn't have anything special to help them. They only had their eyes to see and their hands to measure distances.

The easiest thing to see at night is the moon because it is the brightest object and the nearest. At the beginning of the night, it will be in the east. Because the Earth is spinning, the moon looks like it is moving across the sky, so as the time gets later, the moon will move above you and start to set in the west.

The second brightest object in the sky is the planet Venus. You can also see Mercury, Mars, Jupiter, and Saturn. Mars is easy to spot because it looks a little bit red, and Saturn looks a bit yellow.

You can also see thousands of stars in the sky, and you won't need a telescope to find the constellations. In the next few chapters, you'll find out where they are, what they look like, and how to find them.

One of the most exciting things you can see without a telescope is the International Space Station! This is where astronauts live when they are in space. You can see it moving in the sky just after sunset. The light from the sun reflects off the space station's solar panels and makes it the third brightest object in the night sky. To see when the International Space Station is next passing near you, go to spotthestation.nasa.gov.

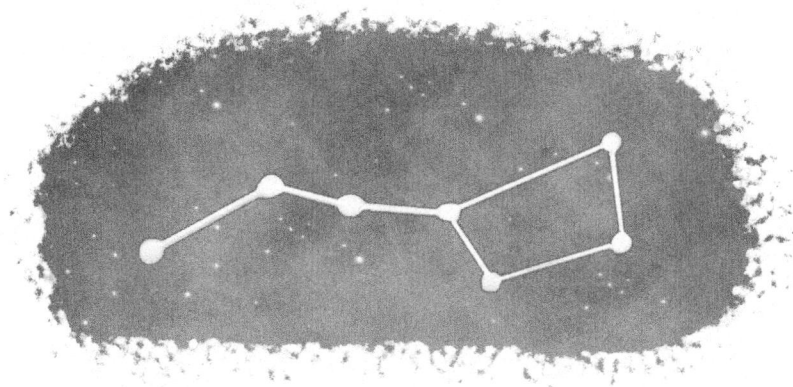

THE BIG DIPPER

Also known as the Plough and the Wagon, the Big Dipper is one of the easiest patterns to find in the night sky. It looks a bit like a saucepan and is made up of seven stars; four in 'the bowl' and three in 'the handle.' The brightest star in the Big Dipper is more than 100 times brighter than our sun, but it's very far away. Nearby is the Little Dipper, a smaller version that is almost the same shape.

Sailors used to use the Big Dipper to navigate at night because it points towards the North Star. Find the two stars at the end of 'the bowl' (these are the two stars furthest to the right in the Big Dipper picture) and draw an imaginary line straight upward through them. Follow that line upward, and you will find a very bright star at the end of the handle of the Little Dipper. These two stars are called the pointer stars because they point to Polaris. Another name for the Big Dipper is Ursa Major, and another name for the Little Dipper is Ursa Minor.

THE TALE OF URSA MAJOR AND URSA MINOR

This epic tale starts with Callisto, a human woman who Zeus's wife, Hera, did not favor. Hera turned poor Callisto into a big grizzly bear. Callisto couldn't go back home to her family and had to live in the woods. Callisto had a son, and she missed him very much. One day, her son went hunting in the woods, and Callisto spotted him from afar. This made her so happy that she ran towards him to give him a big hug, but her son thought she was an ordinary bear coming to attack him! He held up his spear, ready to attack the scary bear.

Zeus was watching all of this from the sky and decided he would help. He picked up Callisto and her son and put them into the stars, where they could always be together. Callisto is Ursa Major—the big bear, and her son is Ursa Minor—the little bear.

A HANDY TIP FROM ASTRONOMERS

Astronomers use a measurement called degrees to show how far apart different objects in space are. You can use them, too, with this amazing trick. All you need is your own hand!

Straighten your arm out in front of you and make your hand into a fist. The distance from your first knuckle (don't count the thumb) to your fourth knuckle is 10 degrees. Now spread out just your thumb and pinkie finger. The distance from tip to tip is 25 degrees. And if you hold up just your pinkie finger, the width of it is 1 degree.

. . .

This handy tip can help you to find the stars. Try it out with Polaris (AKA the North Star)! It should be 30 degrees from the end of the Big Dipper. You can measure this using three fists. Did it work?

POLARIS OR THE NORTH STAR

Polaris is the last star in the Little Dipper, and it is the most important star—apart from our own sun—because it helps us find where north is. Explorers and sailors would use Polaris to make sure they didn't get lost. It is the only star in the sky that doesn't move. In fact, all the other stars look like they're spinning around the North Star.

Polaris is about 70 million years old, which means that some of the dinosaurs would have been able to see it!

FINDING NORTH

You've already learned how to find the Polaris (North Star), but there is another way to find where north is. You can use a compass. Compasses have a needle in the middle that always points to the North Pole. Hold your compass flat in the palm of your hand. Turn around to face the direction the needle is pointing in. Congratulations, you've found north!

If you don't have a compass, you can download a smartphone app that works the same way. Finding north will help you know where to look to find the constellations. If you are facing north, then you also know that east is to your right, west is to your left, and south is behind you.

FIRST STARS TO SPOT

You can use some stars to help you find others. This is another way that Polaris, the North Star, is really useful. Lots of constellations can be found by measuring a number of degrees from Polaris. You just need to use your compass to know which direction to measure in.

You might now know how to find the Big Dipper and the Little Dipper. Remember to look for them in the north.

. . .

Another easy constellation to find is Orion. This time you will have to look to the south. Use the hand method to measure roughly 30 degrees above the horizon and look for three bright stars in a line. These stars make up Orion's Belt. His arms stretch above this belt, and his legs stand below.

If you measure about 40 degrees west from Orion's Belt, you will find a cluster of stars called the Pleiades. This group is made up of about 3,000 stars, all twinkling together. They look like someone spilled a bag of diamonds in the sky. The Pleiades is one of the closest star clusters to Earth, which is why it looks so bright.

CHAPTER 4
CONSTELLATIONS FOR SPRING TIME

Because the Earth is always moving around the sun, we can't always see the same stars in the sky. Just like you see different things when you look out of your car window, the scenery in space changes every day, but because the Earth is moving in an orbit, it will always come back to the same place at the same time. Astronomers have been able to create maps of the stars, so we know what we will be able to see at different times of the year.

These constellations can all be seen in the springtime (as long as it's not raining)!

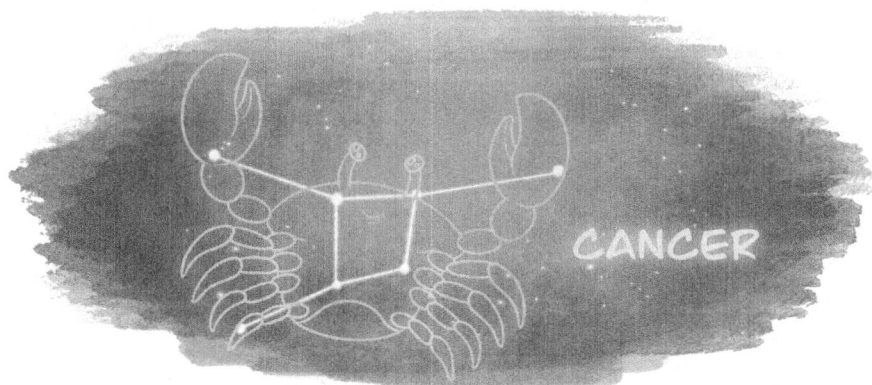

CANCER

The best time to see this crustacean constellation is between February and May. It is quite a hard constellation to spot because the stars within it are not as bright as many others. You will need to remember how to measure degrees with your hands.

First, follow the instructions on the next pages to find the constellation of Leo. Try and imagine a line going along Leo's back, starting with the star at the top of its tail and then joining to the star at the base of its mane. Using your fists to measure 20 degrees, keep drawing that line under Leo's head and out in front of him. You should find the right star in the middle of the crab.

. . .

Another way to find Cancer is to use your compass. Face south and use your fists to measure 50–60 degrees up from the horizon. Depending on the month, you might have to look a little bit more to the left or right. If you combine both of these techniques, you should have a really good chance of spotting it!

Did You Know?

- Cancer was first recorded in 2 AD by a Greek astronomer called Ptolemy.
- This constellation has a star cluster at its center. Called the Beehive Cluster, it has around 1,000 stars and is over 600 million years old.

LEO

Leo, the lion, can be seen roaring across the eastern part of the sky in March, and by May, it's moved to the south. The picture of the lion has been recognized in the sky for more than 6,000 years. It is one of the constellations that are the easiest to see because Leo is made up of some very bright stars.

To find Leo in the sky, you first need to find the Big Dipper. Find the two stars that make up the side of the bowl furthest from the handle. Use your imagination to connect them together and draw a line through them. Keep that line going out of the bottom of the spoon for about 35–40 degrees. Remember, that's three and a half fists! Your line should end at the tip of Leo's tail.

. . .

You can also find Leo using a compass, but the direction you face will change depending on which month it is. In March, face east and measure 40 degrees above the horizon. In April and May, you'll need to measure 60 degrees up and face south to southeast.

Did You Know?

- The constellation of Leo can be seen from both the northern and southern hemispheres.
- Leo is home to 156 different stars, but only 13 of them have been given official names. The brightest star is called Regulus.

THE TALE OF LEO THE LION

Here is a mythological tale that people a long time ago told about the constellation of Leo. The first task given to Hercules involved a lion in the Greek town of Nimea. The lion would go into the town and capture some of the townspeople! When the villagers went to rescue them from the lion's cave, the lion would eat them all up! No one could defeat the lion because its skin was so thick that swords and spears just bounced off it. Hercules fought the lion with his bare hands, defeated it, and freed the captured townspeople.

Zeus's wife, Hera, was upset that the lion had not defeated Hercules, but she wanted to reward it for trying. She put the lion in the stars and made the constellation called Leo.

BOÖTES

There are many different stories about who Boötes was that all come from Greek mythologies. The most famous story tells that Boötes was the man who invented the plough, making farming faster and easier and bringing more food to all the villages. His image was placed in the stars to honor him for his marvelous invention.

If you want to see Boötes for yourself, you'll need to look to the east in April and May, and they turn towards the south in June and July. Don't forget to use a compass or a compass app to make sure you're facing in the right direction. In April, the constellation is only 20 degrees above the horizon, but in the other months, you'll need to measure about 60 degrees.

. . .

You can also find Boötes by using the Big Dipper to help you. Work out where the handle of the Big Dipper is and join the stars up with a curved line. Keep following that imaginary curve for another 30 degrees, and you should find yourself at the brightest star in Boötes. This star is called Arcturus and is like the belly button of Boötes! Below Arcturus, you can see two legs, and above it is the kite-shaped torso of the plowman.

Did You Know?

- The constellation of Boötes contains 10 stars which have planets orbiting around them.
- There is a huge area of space in Boötes called the Boötes Void because it appears to be empty. It contains 60 galaxies, but in an area that big, you would expect to see around 1,000. That's a lot of missing galaxies! Many astronomers think the Boötes void is pretty spooky because it's so dark. Maybe they're worried something is eating the stars?

VIRGO

The constellation of Virgo is the second largest constellation in the sky. Virgo is usually linked with the harvest and may even be the Greek goddess of the harvest herself. She was called Demeter, and she made sure that the crops grew well and everyone had plenty to eat. Some people think that Virgo is not Demeter but her daughter Persephone who brings about the changes in the seasons. Whoever Virgo is, the constellation shows a young lady holding a sheaf of wheat in her left hand to remind everyone that she brings good health to the crops.

Virgo has some faint stars and some bright stars, which means some parts of the constellation are easier to spot than others. You might have to look really hard to see everything. If you know how to find Boötes, you should also be able to find Virgo.

· · ·

Start with the Big Dipper again and imagine a curved line coming out of the handle. Follow that line for 30 degrees— three fists—until you reach the bright star of Arcturus. Keep going for another 30 degrees, and you should find another really bright star. This one is called Spica, and it is the wheat that Virgo is holding.

Another way to find the constellation Virgo is to use a compass to find southeast and measure about 30 degrees above the horizon. Then, look for the bright star of Spica to help you find the rest of the picture. Virgo is best seen between April and June.

Did You Know?

- The constellation of Virgo is home to several galaxies. One of them has been given a really funny name—the Sombrero Galaxy! This is because it is in the shape of a wide hat.
- Spica is a type of star called a blue giant. It is more than 12,000 times brighter than our sun, which is why we can see it from so far away. You should be able to see that it looks bluer than some of the other stars nearby, and this is one way to help you identify it.

CHAPTER 5
CONSTELLATIONS FOR SUMMER TIME

Spotting constellations in summer can be tricky because it doesn't get dark until much later in the day. Of course, the stars are there even in the daytime, but we can't see them because of the light from our sun. The best time to look for constellations is usually about 9:00 p.m., but you might have to stay up even later than that if it isn't dark enough yet!

The good news is that there are plenty of constellations to look for once it does get dark. Here are the summer stars worth missing sleep for.

HERCULES

Hercules is visible in the night sky for five months of the year. In May and June, you can find him due east. In August and September, he will be in the west. And during July, he is right overhead!

The best way to find Hercules is by first spotting two of the brightest stars in the sky. One is Arcturus, the star in the middle of Boötes, and you can check back through this book to remind yourself how to find it. The other star is called Vega. To find Vega, you need to look north-northeast. Draw a line straight up from the horizon to the point right above your head. Vega will be the brightest star on that line.

. . .

Once you've found both Vega and Arcturus, join them up with an imaginary line. Right in the middle of that line should be the Keystone asterism. This is a rhombus of four stars that also acts as Hercules's shorts! You should then be able to also see the arms and legs that make up the rest of the constellation.

You can double-check that you're looking in the right place by measuring from the horizon with your fists. In May and September, measure 3-4 fists. In June and August, measure 5-6 fists. In July, you will need to count out 9 fists.

Did You Know?

- If you have a telescope, you might be able to spot the Great Cluster—a circular group of a million stars. It is on the edge of the Keystone asterism, but even though it has so many stars, it is not very bright.
- There are 29 planets orbiting the stars in Hercules, including a gas giant that is 8 times the size of Jupiter —the largest planet in our solar system.

THE TALE OF HERCULES

The story of Hercules is one of the most famous stories ever told. Hercules's father was Zeus, but his mother was a human woman. Zeus's wife was not happy about this, and she was always doing mean things to Hercules. She made the king send Hercules on 12 impossible tasks, hoping that he would be destroyed. Hercules was very strong and very brave, though, and he finished all his tasks. When he passed away, Zeus made a constellation in his honor. The constellation of Hercules shows him wrestling with the monster Hydra, which was his second task.

LIBRA

The goddess of law in Ancient Greece was called Dike, and she carried a set of weighing scales with her. She would use them to balance up what was fair and just. The constellation of Libra is a picture of those scales, reminding everyone that justice is important.

You can find Libra by facing south in the months of May, June, and July. It always appears pretty low on the horizon, so you'll need to wait until the sun has set fully to be able to see it. Look just above the southern horizon and try to find a bright red star. This star is called Antares. It is between 20–30 degrees up, depending on exactly where you are in the world.

. . .

You will also need to find Spica, the brightest star in Virgo. Once you've spotted both of these stars, try and imagine a line joining them together, and you'll find Libra right in the middle. It's one of the smallest constellations, though, so you might need an expert star-spotter to help you.

Check you're in the right place by measuring 30 degrees above the horizon. There are three stars just above Antares that are in a line like Orion's Belt. Libra is just above those.

Did You Know?

- Libra is the only constellation that gives its name to one of the 12 signs in the zodiac that is not a living creature. All the others are either animals or people.
- The stars of Libra used to be part of the constellation Scorpio. Over the years, they have been recognized as their own constellation but are still very close to Scorpio, and you can use one constellation to help find the other.

CORONA
BOREALIS

CORONA BOREALIS

The Corona Borealis constellation is very small, but because of its shape, it is quite easy to spot. It looks exactly like the object it represents—a shiny, jeweled crown. This crown was given to a princess called Ariadne. It was a wedding present from her husband, the god Dionysus. Dionysus wanted to remember that special day forever, so he made a picture of the crown in the night sky.

You can see Corona Borealis between May and September. It is always near the constellation of Hercules, and you can find it in a similar way. Find the bright stars Vega and Arcturus and imagine a line joining them together. Starting from Arcturus, measure 20 degrees towards Vega, and you should land at another bright star. This is called Alphecca, and it is the brightest star in Corona Borealis. It is at the bottom of the curved crown shape.

Alternatively, you can find Corona Borealis by measuring from the horizon. This can be tricky because it moves around a lot—which is weird, as a crown doesn't have any legs! In May, you need to be facing east and measure 50 degrees (five fists) up from the horizon. In June and July, you need to look more towards the south and measure 70 degrees (seven fists) up from the horizon. In August and September, you should face west and measure at least 30 degrees or three fists.

Did You Know?

- Corona Borealis used to just be called Corona. There is another constellation that looks like a crown called Corona Australis, so the second word was added because people were getting confused. Corona Borealis is the Northern Crown, and Corona Australis is the Southern Crown.
- Corona Borealis only has eight stars in its pattern, and five of them have planets that orbit them.

LYRA
THE HARP

LYRA

You've probably already seen Lyra but didn't realize it since this is the constellation with Vega in its pattern. Because of this, it is really easy to find Lyra, and you can look for it between the months of June and October. Lyra is actually shaped like a little fish with a triangle tail and a parallelogram body.

Remember how to find Vega? Look to the north-northeast and imagine a line joining the horizon to the highest point in the sky. Vega will be the brightest star on that line. Vega is one of the corners of Lyra's triangle, so if you look around, you should be able to identify the rest of the constellation.

If you'd rather find Lyra by measuring, get your compass or compass app ready. In June and July, you'll need to face east. In

September and October, you'll need to be looking west, but in August, you should find Lyra and Vega right over your head. How many degrees you'll have to measure depends on when you are looking. Because Lyra moves overhead, its distance from the horizon changes quickly. In June and October, measure at least 40 degrees up, but in July and September, you'll need to measure at least 60 degrees.

Did You Know?

- Lyra's brightest star, Vega, was the first star other than our sun to have its photograph taken. Astronomers at Harvard College Observatory did this in 1850.
- Vega is a really important star because it used to be the North Star. Because the Earth rotates on a slight angle, the position of the North Pole changes really, *really* slowly. Eventually, it stopped pointing to Vega and pointed to Polaris again instead. Vega will be the North Star again in about 13,000 years.

THE TALE OF LYRA THE HARP

Not all of the constellations are named after animals or people. Lyra was a harp that belonged to the Greek musician Orpheus. Orpheus traveled with Jason on his quest to find the Golden

Fleece and used his harp to help whenever he could. His music had a magical power to calm angry animals and stop them from being dangerous. Zeus made the constellation Lyra out of stars. It was his way of helping everyone remember Orpheus.

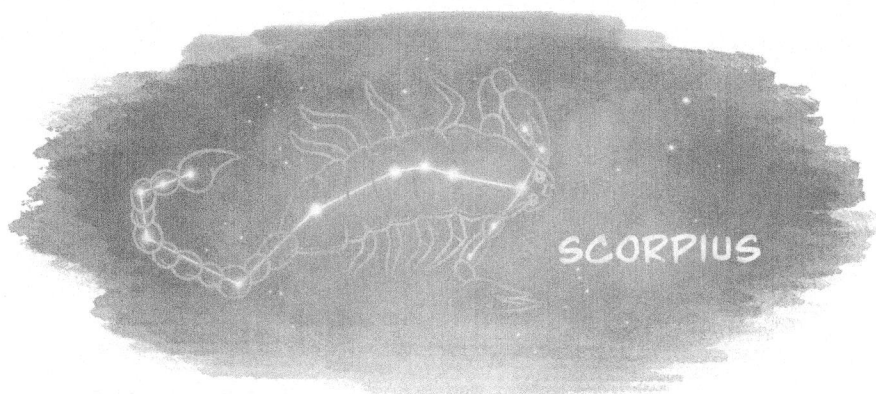

SCORPIUS

This constellation is easier to see if you live in the southern hemisphere, but in the summer, it is possible to spot this sneaky scorpion just peaking over the horizon. You'll have to wait until later in the night to see it, though (around 10:00 p.m.). Your best chance of seeing Scorpius is in July, but you might also be able to spot it in June and August, especially if you live nearer to the equator.

To find Scorpius, face the southern horizon and search for a bright star that looks a little reddish-orange. This is Antares—the same star we used to help us find Libra. On one side of Antares are three stars, all in a line. These make up the claw of the scorpion. On the other side of Antares is a long shape, a bit like a question mark. This is Scorpius's poisonous tail.

· · ·

Did You Know?

- In Hawaii, the curved tail of Scorpius is said to represent Maui's magical fish hook. Maui is a demigod who appears in lots of Hawaiian myths, but most people know him now from the film Moana.
- Antares is sometimes called Mars's Rival because the two look very similar. They can be almost impossible to tell apart when they appear in the sky at the same time. Both have a red tint and look brighter than the rest of the stars around them.

THE TALE OF SCORPIUS THE SCORPION

Here is another amazing mythological constellation legend, this time of Scorpius the Scorpion. Orion was such a great hunter that he once boasted he would hunt every animal in the world. This wasn't a very nice thing to say, and the Greek goddess Gaia—who had created all of nature—was very angry with him. She made Scorpius the giant scorpion to protect her animals. Scorpius fought with Orion and managed to defeat him. Zeus was so impressed with Scorpius that he gave him his own spot in the sky as a constellation. There he stayed as a reminder to Orion that it is not a good idea to be boastful.

Orion and Scorpius can never be seen in the sky at the same time. The Greeks said this is because when one appears, he chases the other away. We know now that it is because the Earth is rotating, and the two constellations are at different places in space.

CYGNUS

Later on, you'll discover how the Greek god Zeus changed himself into a bull when he met the princess Europa. However, the constellation Cygnus tells us about another folklore tale where Zeus, again, wanted to get someone's attention by turning into a creature. This time he became a swan, and the person's attention he was trying to get was called Leda, the mother of Castor and Pollux.

Cygnus can be seen flying through the sky between July and October. You'll need to find Vega again, so you must be getting good at this by now! Once you can see Vega, imagine a line that joins it to the northeast horizon. Measure 25 degrees along this line, and you'll pass by the star at the very end of Cygnus's tail. It is called Deneb, and it is also part of an asterism called the

Northern Cross. If you extend the lines of the Northern Cross, you will make two wings and the long neck of the swan.

If you go searching in September, you'll be able to see Cygnus flying right above you. In July and August, you will need to face east and measure 40–70 degrees from the horizon, depending on how early you are looking. In October, you should look west and measure about 60 degrees up from the horizon. Because Cygnus has such a distinctive cross at its center, it is one of the easiest constellations to spot.

<u>Did You Know?</u>

- If you are stargazing from a very dark area, you might be able to see what looks like a thin, milky cloud underneath Cygnus. This is part of the Milky Way, our amazing galaxy.
- If you have binoculars or a telescope, you might also be able to see the North American Nebula. It is a giant cloud of space dust and looks like a faint glow next to the star Deneb.

CHAPTER 5

AQUILA

AQUILA

Another mythological bird in the stars, Aquila, is an eagle that flies close to Cygnus. The eagle belonged to Zeus and was the only other animal apart from Pegasus who could carry his lightning bolts. Aquila was also told by Zeus to bring a human called Ganymede up to Mount Olympus—the home of the gods—to serve them and do all of their chores. Ganymede would eventually be turned into his own constellation called Aquarius.

Aquila can be seen in July, August, September, and October. In July, start by using your compass or compass app to find east and then measure three fists up from the horizon. Face slightly more south in August and look a bit higher—five fists this time. In September and October, you'll have to find the southwestern sky and look between four and five fists above the horizon.

. . .

You can also find Aquila by searching for Vega. Imagine a line going between Vega and the star at the end of the parallelogram of Lyra. Go three fists along this line, and you should see the brightest star at the head of Aquila. This star is called Altair, and it has smaller stars on each side, like little ears.

Did You Know?

- If you join Aquila's bright star, Altair, with Vega and Deneb, you will make another asterism. This asterism is called the Summer Triangle.
- Aquila is the Latin word for eagle, and Altair comes from an Arabic phrase meaning "flying eagle." This constellation has an eagle inside an eagle!

SAGITTARIUS

Sagittarius is another constellation that stays close to the horizon, never getting higher than 20 degrees. This means you'll need it to be very dark outside, and you might only be able to see part of this mythical archer. The only time to see Sagittarius in the northern hemisphere is from July to September.

Face the south and use the tips on the previous pages for finding Altair. Use your fists to measure 40 degrees from Altair to the southwestern horizon. You should now be near a special group of stars in Sagittarius: the Teapot asterism. This asterism is the chest and arms of the archer as he pulls back his bow, ready to fire toward the nearby Scorpius.

. . .

If you want to find Sagittarius using your compass or compass app, you need to find and face south. Measure 10–20 degrees up from the horizon, and keep looking for that teapot shape.

Did You Know?

- Although you can see Sagittarius in the northern hemisphere, it is more commonly thought of as a southern hemisphere constellation. It is actually the largest southern hemisphere constellation but only the 15th largest constellation overall.
- Sagittarius is at the center of the Milky Way galaxy. This explains why there are so many star clusters and nebulae within the constellation.

THE TALE OF SAGITTARIUS

Here is another handed-down legendary tale. The constellation of Sagittarius is supposed to represent Chiron, who was an archer in Greek mythology, but he was extra special because he was also a centaur (a mythological creature). A centaur has the body of a horse, but where the horse's neck should be is the torso, arms, and head of a man. Centaurs were supposed to be very wise, and Chiron was the wisest of them all. He taught many great heroes like Hercules, Jason, and Achilles.

One day there was an accident, and Chiron became really unwell because he was poisoned by the Hydra that Hercules defeated. Even though Chiron was a skilled healer, he couldn't stop the poison from making him unwell. So, Zeus lifted Chiron up and put him in the stars, where he could stay forever and not be sick anymore.

CHAPTER 6
CONSTELLATIONS FOR FALL TIME

As the days start getting shorter, you have longer night times to spend stargazing. The stars that you saw in the spring are now as far away as they can be, and a completely new set of stars twinkle in the sky.

PEGASUS

The mighty winged horse is a good constellation to find. It has an easily recognizable shape, including an asterism in the shape of a square. The neck and head of Pegasus start at one corner of this square from a star called Markab. Two front legs come out of another star called Scheat. You can see Pegasus in the sky from September all the way through to December.

Use your compass to find the eastern horizon, and measure 30 degrees up in September and 60 degrees up in October. You should be able to see the Great Square asterism because the four stars at the corners are very bright. If you're looking in November, remember to face south instead of east and measure 70 degrees up. In December, Pegasus moves all the way round to the west and can be found 50 degrees up.

· · ·

You can also find Pegasus if you know where the North Star is. You can find it by locating the Big Dipper and following the pointer stars. Imagine a line from the end of the Big Dipper's handle to Polaris. Measure twice as far again, and you should reach a group of stars that make a W shape. Find the brightest star at the end of this W and draw another line from Polaris that goes through it. This line will take you to the Great Square of Pegasus.

Did You Know?

- Because the Great Square is so easy to spot, it is used by navigators and astronomers to help find other features in space.
- The first planet to be discovered outside our solar system is orbiting a star in Pegasus.

THE TALE OF PEGASUS THE WINGED HORSE

Here is the fable of the mighty Pegasus. Pegasus belonged to a Greek hero called Bellerophon. Together they went on many adventures. Pegasus helped Bellerophon fight a terrible monster called the Chimera. It was part lion, part goat, and part snake, and it breathed fire.

. . .

Pegasus was a very special horse, and not just because it had wings and could fly. If it stamped its hoof on the ground, water would shoot up in a jet, and if Pegasus clapped its wings together like we clap our hands, it would make the sound of thunder. Pegasus was also the only animal that could carry Zeus's lightning bolts without getting hurt. Zeus would often borrow Pegasus to help him out, and he decided to make a constellation to honor Pegasus for being so loyal and helpful.

CAPRICORN

When the Greek philosopher Ptolemy wrote down the stories of all the constellations, he said that Capricorn was the image of the Greek god Pan. Pan was a man with goat's horns and legs. In one story, Pan was being chased by a monster and had to jump into a river to escape. When his legs got wet, they changed into a fish's tail.

The constellation of Capricorn is really difficult to see with just your eyes because the stars that make up this picture are very faint. If you want to catch a glimpse of the mythical half-goat half-fish, you'll need to find somewhere very dark and far away from artificial light. Capricorn is visible between September and November.

·   ·   ·

Make sure you're facing south and look for the bright stars Vega and Altair. These stars are in the constellations of Lyra and Aquila. Starting at Altair, imagine a line going through Vega. Measure three fists (30 degrees) from Vega, and you should land on the constellation of Capricorn.

Another way to find Capricorn is to measure 30 degrees up from the southern horizon. Look slightly east in September and slightly west in October.

<u>**Did You Know?**</u>

- The star in Capricorn's horns called Algedi is actually two stars! These stars orbit each other, and you can see the separate stars with a pair of binoculars.
- Most constellations were first written down by the Ancient Greeks, but Capricorn seems to have been designed by the Babylonians. Ancient relics with pictures of a goat with a fish tail have been found that are 4,000 years old.

AQUARIUS

Remember Ganymede, the young man taken up to Mount Olympus by the eagle Aquila that we talked about earlier? Well, he is the constellation Aquarius. The tale goes that in return for bringing the gods drinks and filling their cups when they were thirsty, Ganymede was promised that he would never get old. Zeus put him up in the stars so that he would always be there.

You can try and spot this constellation between September and November, but it might take a lot of practice because Aquarius doesn't have any bright stars. It is very close to Capricorn and Pisces, so you can use these other constellations to help you.

Like the ancient astronomers, you can use the Great Square of Pegasus to help you find Aquarius. Find the star Scheat, which is the corner of the square with the legs of Pegasus. Draw a line from this star to Markab, the star at the base of Pegasus's neck. Keep that line going through Markab for 20 degrees, and you should land on Aquarius.

You can also find Aquarius by facing south—don't forget to use a compass or compass app to help you. Measure 30 degrees up from the horizon. Look southeast in September and southwest in November to follow Aquarius across the night sky.

Did You Know?

- The name Aquarius comes from the Latin word *aqua,* meaning water. In the stars, Aquarius can be seen pouring water from a jug.
- Aquarius is one of several constellations with a water theme. These are found in an area of space known as "The Sea."

CASSIOPEIA

The fable of Queen Cassiopeia contains Greek Gods and sea monsters! Queen Cassiopeia once boasted that she was even more beautiful than Poseidon's daughters. Poseidon, the Greek god of the sea, was not very happy with her claims and sent a sea serpent to attack her kingdom. After Cassiopeia's defeat, she was placed in the stars as punishment for being so vain. In her constellation, she is chained to a giant throne, and for half the year, she has to hang upside down.

The constellation of Cassiopeia is one of the few constellations that is visible all year round, but the best time to see it is between September and February. Cassiopeia is near the North Star. Find the Big Dipper and draw a line from the pointer stars to Polaris. Keep the line going for the same distance again, and you will land on Cassiopeia. The five stars of Cassiopeia are shaped like a W or M, depending on which way up it is. All five stars are very bright, so they should be easy to spot.

Cassiopeia is found in the northern directions during the fall and winter months, so you can use a compass to make sure you're looking in the right direction. Look to the northeast in September, turn north for November, and northwest in January. The constellation rises and falls overhead, so you'll find it 30–40 degrees high in September and February, rising up to 70 degrees in November.

Did You Know?

- All five of the stars in Cassiopeia have official names. They are Segin, Ruchbah, Gamma, Schedar, and Caph. Schedar looks orange, while all the others appear white.
- The constellation used to be called Cassiopeia's Chair because of the throne she is tied to. The name was only changed in 1930.

ARIES

The mythological tale of Aries states that he was a special ram with a beautiful golden fleece. He was offered as a tribute to Zeus, and Zeus placed the ram in the stars. Aries's Golden Fleece was guarded by a dragon. The hero Jason was sent to recover it.

This constellation is best seen between October and January, and even then, it can be tricky to spot. Look out for the brightest star, Hamal, to help you. Aries is shaped like a straight line with a slight bend on the end, and Hamal is in the middle.

The easiest way to find Aries is to first look for Cassiopeia. Find the two stars called Caph and Shedar. Remember, Shedar is easy to spot because it has a yellow-orange tint. Draw a line between the two and follow it beyond Shedar by 40 degrees. This will take you to the constellation of Aries.

Finding Aries with your compass is harder because it moves a lot between the months. In October, face east and measure 30 degrees up. In November, face southeast and measure 70 degrees up. In December, you'll still measure 70 degrees up, but this time, you need to make sure you're facing south. In January, you will have to face to the west and measure 50 degrees up from the horizon.

Did You Know?

- Aries is home to a spiral galaxy that is 450 million light years away from Earth.
- 2,000 years before the Greeks named Aries, the constellation was already imagined to be the shape of a ram by Babylonian astronomers.

PISCES

Pisces is the Latin word for fish, and there are two fish in this constellation. The story goes that the constellation represents two fish that saved the goddess Aphrodite and her son Eros when they were being chased by a monster. They jumped into a river to escape, and two fish swam over and helped them to safety.

This is another tricky constellation to spot because there are no bright stars in Pisces. The constellation is a large V shape with a star at the point, which joins the tails of the two fish together. This star is called Alrescha.

The best time to spot Pisces is between October and January. You can use the Great Square to help you find Pisces. If you measure 10 degrees to the east of the Great Square, you should land on one of the fish, and if you measure 10 degrees to the south, you should find the other. Alrescha is 20 degrees to the southeast.

In October, find the eastern horizon with your compass and measure up 30 degrees to find Pisces. Do the same in January but facing west. In November and December, you'll need to face south and measure up 60–70 degrees.

Did You Know?

- Pisces is in the area of the sky known as "The Sea," along with other water-themed constellations like Aquarius and Capricorn.
- Thirteen of the stars in Pisces have their own planets.

CHAPTER 7
CONSTELLATIONS FOR WINTER TIME

Winter isn't always the easiest time to see constellations, which is a shame, as some are only visible during these months. Bad weather means that the skies are often cloudy and the stars are obscured. However, if you do manage to find a clear day, there are some great constellations to spot.

TAURUS

The bull Taurus can be seen rampaging across both the northern and southern hemispheres but at different times of the year. You can see it best between December and March by looking towards the south.

Taurus is very close to the constellation of Orion. If you draw an imaginary line through the stars on Orion's belt and keep following it west for an extra 30 degrees, you will reach the head of the bull. The head is a small triangle with two long horns coming out of the top. If you keep following your line for an extra 10 degrees, you will come to a star cluster called The Pleiades.

· · ·

Taurus is lower in the sky in December and March, so you'll need to measure 40–50 degrees from the southern horizon. Look a little to the east in December and January and a little to the west in March. In January and February, you'll have to measure 60–70 degrees up as the stars rise higher.

Did You Know?

- The constellation of Taurus has been drawn as a bull for more than 10,000 years! Pictures of this arrangement have been found in cave paintings.
- Taurus and Orion face each other as if they are in battle. This makes sense because Orion is a great hunter.

THE TALE OF TAURUS THE BULL

In this magical story, Zeus became interested in a human princess called Europa and wanted her to like him too. Because humans can only see gods when they are in disguise, Zeus decided to turn himself into a giant white bull. He went to Europa when she was gathering flowers on the shore. Europa had never seen such a friendly bull before, and she climbed on Zeus's back. He plunged into the sea and swam all the way to the island of Crete with Europa still riding on his back.

Zeus changed into a man and told Europa who he was. She stayed on the island, and they started a family together. Because Zeus was a god, he didn't get older, but Europa did. When she passed away, Zeus was very sad, so he turned into the bull one more time and carried Europa up to the stars, where they became the constellation Taurus the Bull.

ORION

Orion is one of the most famous constellations and is also one of the easiest to spot. The distinctive belt of three bright stars means it can even be seen when the sky is not very dark. Although you can see Orion at many times of the year, the best time to spot the constellation is from January to March.

Finding Orion with a compass is quite easy. Use it to help you find the southern horizon and measure up. In January, you'll have to look slightly to the east and measure 30 degrees. In March, look slightly to the west and measure 40 degrees. In February, the constellation is at its highest, so you will need to measure 50 degrees.

. . .

You can also find Orion without measuring because of how bright Orion's Belt is. Face south and look up until you see three bright stars all in a line. Orion's shoulders rise up from the belt. Look out for the bright star called Betelgeuse in his armpit! Orion's knees are the same distance below the belt, and the bright star on one knee is Rigel.

Did You Know?

- Orion's Belt is an asterism that has been recognized for thousands of years. The Ancient Egyptians designed their pyramids, so they would point to this asterism.
- Underneath Orion's Belt is the Orion Nebula, but you can't see it without using a powerful telescope because it is very far away.

THE TALE BEHIND ORION

This is the old legend of Orion, a hunter who lived with Artemis, the Greek goddess of the forest and wild animals. Orion was a demigod, and his dad was Poseidon, the Greek god of the sea. Orion and Artemis were in love and wanted to get married, but her brother, Apollo, did not want this to happen. He decided to play a trick on Artemis. She was also a very good hunter, and Apollo dared her to fire an arrow and hit a small target in the lake. The lake was very far away. However, Artemis was an excellent shot, and her arrow hit the target.

When she went to see what she had hit, she was upset to see it was Orion, who had been swimming in the lake. Not wanting to forget him, Artemis put his image in the stars, where he is shown with his hunting club held high.

GEMINI

The stars that make up the heads of Castor and Pollux are bright and easy to spot, but being able to see the rest of the constellation Gemini requires a very dark sky because the stars are much fainter. Your best chance to see the celestial twins is between January and April.

First, find Orion's Belt and the neighboring stars Betelgeuse and Rigel. If you imagine a line from Betelgeuse going all the way through Rigel and a further 30 degrees, you should find yourself near two fairly bright stars. Named after the twins, the brighter one is Pollux, and the other is Castor.

If you can't see Orion, you can try and find Gemini by measuring degrees from the horizon. In January, face east and measure 40 degrees high. In February, March, and April, you will need to face roughly south and measure about 60–70 degrees high. Once you have spotted the two twin stars, you should look for two stick figure bodies lying parallel with the brightest stars as the heads.

Did You Know?

- Castor is actually a whole system of 6 stars that are so close together that they look like one star.
- The star Castor looks bluish-white, and Pollux looks yellow-orange. This is how you can tell them apart. Maybe the twins aren't identical after all!

THE TALE OF GEMINI

Gemini's famous legend contains identical twins! The constellation of Gemini is named after Castor and Pollux, twin sons of the Queen of Thebes. They looked absolutely identical; however, Castor's dad was the king, and Pollux's dad was Zeus. This made Pollux immortal, which meant that he could live forever.

Castor and Pollux did everything together, including going on adventures. They helped a hero called Jason to find the golden fleece of Aries the ram. The twins had a sister called Helen, who was the most beautiful woman on Earth. One day, Helen was captured and taken to the city of Troy. Her brothers fought in the war to get her back, but Castor was defeated. Pollux didn't want to keep living without his brother and asked Zeus to bring Castor back.

Even Zeus, the king of the gods, could not bring someone back from defeat in battle, but he reunited the twins by placing them both in the night sky. The constellation Gemini looks like two stick men, each with a star as its head. One star is called Castor, and the other star is called Pollux.

CANIS MAJOR

Canis Major is Latin for "greater dog," and this constellation represents one of Orion's hunting dogs. Canis Major can be seen following Orion around the sky. It also looks like it is chasing another constellation called Lepus, which looks like a rabbit or hare. Canis Major is an important constellation because it is home to the brightest star in the sky: Sirius–sometimes called the "Dog Star."

Canis Major never gets very high in the sky, making it a bit tricky to spot. You can only see it in the northern hemisphere in February, March, and April.

Orion can help you to find Canis Major. Look for Orion's Belt and imagine joining up the three stars. Continue that line towards the southeast and measure two fists or 20 degrees. You should come very close to Sirius, which sits on Canis Major's collar like a shiny tag.

If you face the south and measure 3 fists, or 30 degrees, up from the horizon, you should also find Canis Major. Look a little to the east in February and a little to the west in April.

Did You Know?

- Sirius only looks like the brightest star in the sky because it is so close to Earth—only 8.6 light years away. It doesn't actually shine that brightly compared to some of the other stars.
- There is another "dog" constellation in the sky called Canis Minor, which means "lesser dog" in Latin.

CHAPTER 8
INCREDIBLE EVENTS IN THE SKY!

Now that you know the best times of year to see certain constellations, you might also like to watch out for some of the other exciting things that happen in space.

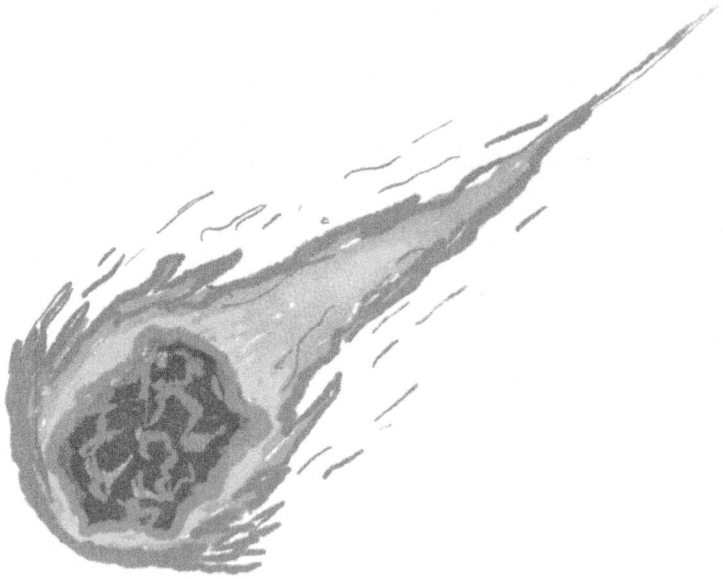

COMETS

Comets orbit the sun just like the planets, but they are much, much smaller. They are mainly made up of ice, but they also have bits of rock and gas in them, too. As they fly around in space, they drop lots of pieces off and leave clouds of space dust. This dust appears like a long, fuzzy tail that trails behind each comet. The head of the comet burns brightly, and most are easy to see using only your eyes.

· · ·

Comets take a lot longer to orbit around the sun than we do because they are further away—even further away than Neptune. Some comets take hundreds of years to complete their orbit. The most famous comet is called Halley's Comet, and it takes around 76 years to make one circle of the sun.

When some comets, like Halley's Comet, fly past the Earth, we are able to see them. This doesn't happen very often, which makes it really exciting when one appears. Halley's Comet won't be visible from Earth again until 2061, and many people who saw it in 1986 won't be around to see it again.

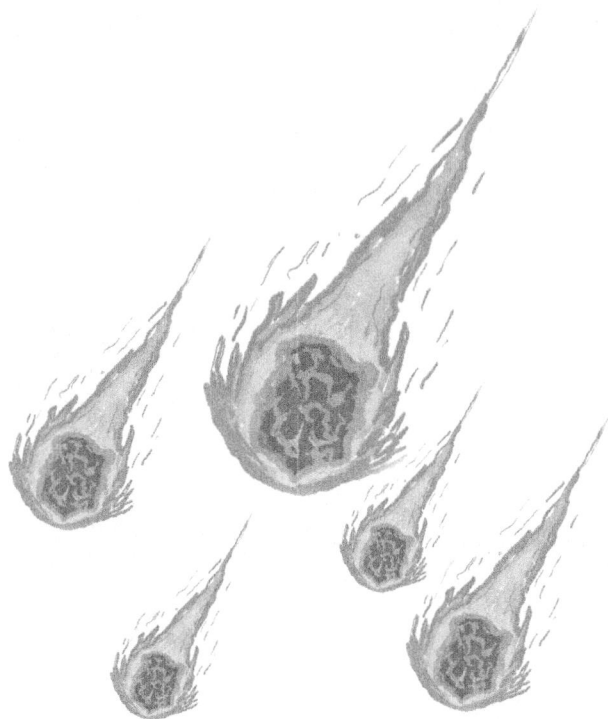

METEOR SHOWERS

You already know that meteors are small pieces of space rock or dust, but I bet you didn't know just how many meteors crash through the Earth's atmosphere every year. Meteor showers are like massive fireworks displays where loads of meteors appear over the course of several days.

·   ·   ·

Meteors are created by comets. When the Earth's orbit passes through a stream of space dust left by a comet, the dust and rocks that enter the atmosphere heat up so quickly that they burn brightly and look like shooting stars.

Because the Earth moves through the same clouds of dust every time it goes around the sun, astronomers are able to tell everyone when the meteor showers will happen. There are hundreds of meteors hitting the Earth every day, even when it isn't nighttime, but you'd have to be looking at exactly the right time to spot one.

If you want to watch a meteor shower, check the best days by using a website like timeanddate.com. Find yourself somewhere in the countryside, well away from towns or cities, which give off lots of light. Make sure you have a clear view of the sky, lie down on something comfy, and wait.

HERE ARE SOME FAMOUS METEOR SHOWERS:

- The Quadrantids shower happens in the first two weeks of January every year. At its peak, you can see up to 110 meteors every hour! They originate close to the constellation Boötes, and this is why they are sometimes called the Boötids.
- The Lyrids start near the constellation Lyra, and they happen in the middle of April. You can see them from both the northern and southern hemispheres. You will have to be patient, though, because even on its best days, you probably won't see more than 18 meteors per hour.
- The Perseids meteor shower is the brightest of the year and lasts for most of July and August. The best time to watch is the second week of August when you can see up to 100 meteors streaming across the sky every hour. The Perseids seem to come from the constellation Perseus, but they are actually the cloud of a comet called Swift-Tuttle.
- The Leonids blast out of the constellation Leo every November and are best viewed in the middle of the month. Even then, you will probably only see one meteor every five minutes.

TOTAL ECLIPSE OF THE MOON

The moon is the brightest object in the night sky, so it's pretty hard to miss. Have you ever noticed that the moon changes shape? Sometimes it even disappears altogether. This happens when the Earth gets caught between the sun and the moon, and the light from the sun gets blocked. It only happens during a full moon and usually only twice a year. However, you won't be able to see all the lunar eclipses because they are only visible from certain places on the planet.

There are two types of lunar eclipses. A total lunar eclipse happens when the moon completely disappears for a few minutes. This means that the Earth has entirely blocked the light from the sun. A partial lunar eclipse happens when the Earth isn't completely between the sun and the moon. When this happens, you'll see the shadow pass over the face of the moon like someone is taking a bite out of it.

CHAPTER 9
DID YOU KNOW HOW AMAZING THE MOON IS?

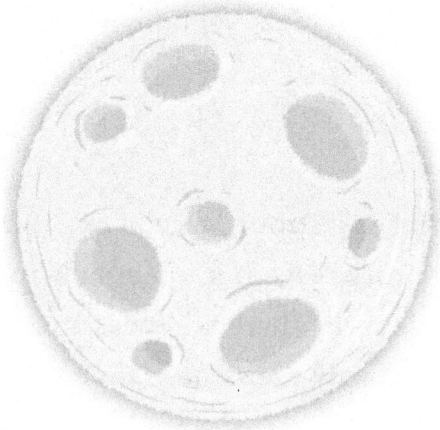

Because the moon is always there, it can be easy to take it for granted, but it's actually really special. The moon is the only natural thing orbiting Earth, and it has been there for 4.6

billion years! That's 1 billion years before the first living things appeared on Earth.

WHERE DID THE MOON COME FROM?

It's very difficult for scientists to know exactly where the moon came from because no one was around to see it first appear. Their best guess is that the moon is actually made of pieces of Earth! Billions of years ago, the Earth was probably hit by a large object the size of a smaller planet. This caused the Earth to break, and bits went flying off into space. The other planet would have been completely broken up, too (like crumbling a cookie), and these bits of dust would have been floating around in space.

Because the Earth has a strong force of gravity, it started to pull these crumbs and rocks together, eventually making the moon. This theory explains why there are rocks, metals, and gasses on the moon that are exactly the same as on Earth.

MOON MICE? ABSOLUTE LUNA-SEA!

Because we can see that the surface of the moon is full of bumps and patches, people used to joke that it was made of cheese! Have you ever seen a slice of Swiss cheese? It is crumbly and full of holes and looks just like the moon, only yellow.

Sadly, the moon is actually made of rock, which is not as tasty. It also has features like the Earth with mountains and seas, and scientists have even given them all names. The most famous is the Sea of Tranquility which is where the astronauts Neil Armstrong and Buzz Aldrin landed when they visited the moon in 1969.

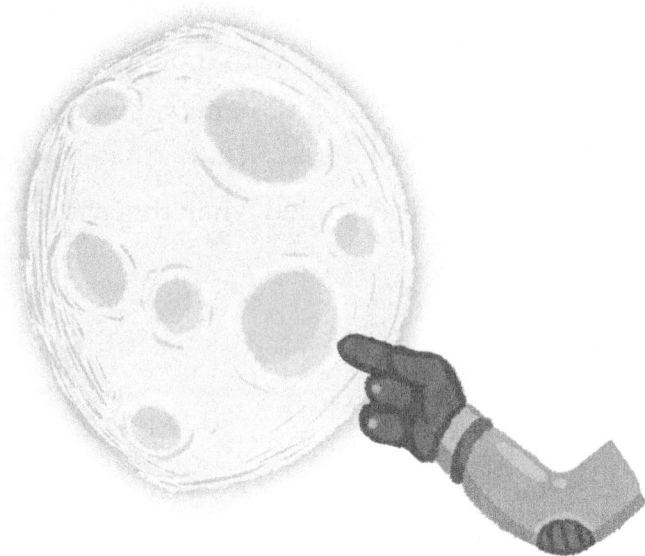

CRATERS

The bumps and holes you can see on the moon are called craters. They are like large bowls, and they make up more than 80% of the moon's surface. Have you ever dropped stones into a sandbox or the sand on the beach? Those stones leave little craters and dips in the sand when they hit it. The craters on the moon were formed when meteors and other space debris crashed into the moon.

MOUNTAINS

In between the moon's craters, you can find some really tall mountains. They were also made by the impact of rocks hitting the moon. When a meteor hits the moon, it pushes the rock and dust out of the way. Some of it gets squashed down, but other bits get shoved to the side of the crater. This makes the sides bigger, and if a lot of rock and dust is pushed to the side, it makes a mountain. The tallest mountain on the moon is called Mons Huygens, and it is 5.5 kilometers tall. This is about the same height as Mount Saint Elias in Alaska.

MARIA

The dark, flat parts of the moon are called the maria, another word for seas. The first astronomers to look at the moon with a telescope thought that these maria looked like they were made of water. However, this turned out to be a mistake because there is no water on the moon.

The maria are flat because they used to be covered in lava. This was probably made in the center of the moon when all the dust and bits of Earth were being pushed together. There is no lava there now. It has cooled down and turned into a type of rock called basalt. Robots have visited the moon and brought some of these basalt rocks back to Earth for scientists to investigate. Scientists are very excited by moon rocks and have collected about 400 kg of samples. That's roughly how much an American crocodile weighs!

LUNAR PHASES AND ORBITS

The moon orbits around the Earth just like all of the planets orbit around the sun. It takes roughly 28 days for the moon to make it all the way around the Earth and back to where it started. The moon also spins on its axis. It takes about 28 days for the moon to make one full rotation. Because it takes the same amount of time for the moon to spin around as it does for it to go around the Earth, the same side of the moon is always facing the planet. This is why, no matter where the moon is in the sky, the pattern on its surface is always the same.

· · ·

During its 28-day cycle, the moon changes shape. This happens because the light from the sun hits different parts of the moon. Sometimes the light shines on the side of the moon that we can't see from Earth, and this makes the moon look dark. Try shining a flashlight on an orange, slowly moving the light in a circle around the fruit.

The moon has five different stages in its cycle:

- Full moon: This is when the moon looks completely round, and we can see all sides of the circle.
- Gibbous moon: The moon looks squished on one side as it becomes covered in shadow.
- Quarter moon: Only half of the moon is visible. The rest is dark. Why is it called a quarter moon and not a half moon? Because the other side of the moon—the one facing away from Earth—is also dark. This means the moon has one-quarter in the light and three-quarters in shadow.
- Crescent moon: This is the moon shape we often see in pictures, where it looks like a smile on its side.
- New moon: This is the thinnest slice of the moon, and it is often so dark that we cannot see it by using just our eyes. It only lasts for a day or two, so the moon isn't gone for long.

. . .

The moon takes two weeks to go from a full moon to a new moon. When the area of the moon that reflects the sun's light gets smaller, we say that the moon is waning. It takes another two weeks for the moon to go from a new moon back to a full moon. During this time, the shadows covering the moon get smaller, and the lighter side gets larger. We call this the waxing moon.

MOON VISITORS

Because the moon is the nearest space object to Earth, it is the easiest for scientists to send spacecraft to. Some of these rockets have had astronauts in them, some have had robots, and others have just flown close by and taken photos.

CHAPTER 9

Back in the 1950s, both the United States and Russia really wanted to be the first country to land on the moon. They both built a lot of rockets and made new designs that they hoped would be able to make the long journey. This time in history is known as the Space Race.

Russia made the first spacecraft to take a picture of the far side of the moon. They also made the first landing on the moon's surface. Neither of these spacecraft had any people inside, though. They were controlled by pilots back on Earth.

The United States was the first country to send astronauts to the moon. The first spaceship just flew around the moon. It was called Apollo 8. Seven months later, a spacecraft called Apollo 11 successfully landed on the moon, and two astronauts, Neil Armstrong and Buzz Aldrin got out and walked around.

Over the next few years, both countries sent robots to the moon. These robots took photographs and videos and collected rock samples. The newest robot on the moon was put there by the Chinese space program in 2019.

CONCLUSION

Good work! You've unlocked many secrets of the stars and are ready to impress your friends with your knowledge of the constellations. From the giant Virgo to the much smaller Corona Borealis, you know all the tips and tricks to find them as well as some amazing facts that will make you sound like a professional astronomer.

There are 24 constellations mentioned in this book. Have you managed to spot them all? Hopefully, you've had lots of fun learning about the wonderful pictures that ancient civilizations saw in the stars, but your adventures in space don't have to end here. There are 88 constellations in total, and now that you know how to navigate the night skies, you are ready to find the rest. You can use a brilliant app like Stellarium to see all the constellations in the sky all around you.

While you're looking to the stars, don't forget there are plenty of other objects to find as well. Watch out for the different phases of the moon, some planets pretending to be stars, and maybe even a magical meteor shower! There are so many things in space to explore that not even scientists know exactly what is out there. Who knows what they (or you!) will discover in the future? Happy stargazing!

GLOSSARY

Some of the words used in this book might be new to you. You can find out what they mean here.

Asterism: A pattern formed in the night sky by joining stars together. Smaller than a constellation.

Astronomer: A type of scientist who studies things in space.

Axis: An imaginary line through the middle of something in which an object rotates around.

Constellation: A group of stars that make a pattern. There are 88 official constellations.

Degree: The unit used to measure the size of an angle.

Equator: An imaginary line around the middle of the Earth.

Galaxy: Many stars grouped together by the force of gravity.

Gravity: A force coming from inside a large object which attracts smaller objects towards it.

Hemisphere: Half of the Earth. The equator divides the Earth into the northern and southern hemispheres.

Planet: A large object in space that orbits around a star.

Meteor: A small space rock that enters the Earth's atmosphere and burns up, creating a bright streak.

Nebula: A cloud of dust or gas in space.

Orbit: The path taken by an object moving in a circle or oval around another, larger object.

Star: A ball of gas that gives out its own light. The sun is our nearest star.

YOUR FEEDBACK IS VALUED!

You know what's even "cooler" than the planet Neptune?

What's that?

When we get feedback from awesome readers like you! We'd love it if you would consider leaving an honest review for this book on Amazon or Audible.

Ok, good to know that we can help!

Thank you, and happy stargazing!

As an independent publishing team floating through space, it would mean the UNIVERSE to get your feedback. It will help us create better books for you and help educate other space travelers even more!

Aniela Publications

Printed in Dunstable, United Kingdom